Bob Forsch's Tales from the Cardinals Dugout

Bob Forsch
with
Tom Wheatley

Sports Publishing L.L.C.
www.SportsPublishingLLC.com

Direction of production: Susan M. Moyer
Project manager: Greg Hickman
Developmental editor: Mark E. Zulauf
Copy editor: Cynthia L. McNew
Dust jacket design: Kerri Baker

ISBN: 1-58261-671-X

Printed in the United States.

SPORTS PUBLISHING L.L.C.
www.SportsPublishingLLC.com

Contents

Introduction

There's nothing like sitting in the dugout to watch a ballgame. That's one thing you really miss when you retire.

The new Cardinals owners invited me down to the dugout at Busch Stadium when they gave Jose Jimenez a watch for pitching his no-hitter. He threw his on June 25, 1999, in Arizona.

I had thrown the last no-hitter for the Cardinals on September 26, 1983. So when the team came back from Arizona, I was part of the pregame ceremony for Jimenez.

He got a Rolex watch. I got a silver platter for my no-hitter, and it was the second one I'd thrown!

But I wasn't complaining. I got to sit in the front row next to the dugout, the end down by first base.

It was incredible to see how fast the game was. It just seemed like everybody threw hard and everybody ran hard. When you watch games on TV, you lose perspective. But if you're real close to the action, you realize how fast the ball gets from the pitcher's hand to home plate. And how fast the batters get down the line to first base when they hit the ball. And how quick the infielders are. And how much ground the outfielders cover.

When you're sitting there, you're 30 years old again.

When I sat in the dugout, back when I really was 30 years old, the game never seemed that fast. But at 45 years old, sitting next to the dugout, it seemed fast.

Real fast.

But through the years, one thing never changes. The dugout is always the best seat in the house.

HUMOR ME

Mike Roarke came over from the Cubs in '83 to be our pitching coach in St. Louis. Hub Kittle had left, and Mike came in to help Bruce Sutter with his split-fingered fastball.

We were in Los Angeles, and John Stuper was starting the game, and he was wild. He walked the bases loaded, and Mike had been out there to the mound once to talk to him.

Then "Stupe" walked in a run, and Whitey went out to get him out of there.

I was in the dugout next to Mike, and I didn't know him that well yet. But I looked at him and said, "Why's Whitey taking him out?"

Mike was ticked already, because his pitcher started out by walking everybody, and he looked at me and said, "What are you talking about?"

I said, "How can you take him out? He's got a no-hitter going!"

Mike didn't say anything. He had this look in his eyes like, "Are you the dumbest person in the world?"

A minute later, he started laughing. He finally figured out who he was dealing with.

JUST DUCKY

In 1968, I went from Hiram Johnson High School in Sacramento—that's Hiram "W." Johnson, and I have no idea who he was—to rookie ball with the Cardinals in Sarasota, Florida.

I was a third baseman-outfielder then. And Ducky Medwick was my hitting coach in rookie ball.

I was hitting a buck-fifty in rookie ball, and I was looking for any help I could get. So Ducky took me to the side and found this bat. I'd never seen anything like it. You didn't know which end you should use, it was so thick.

Apparently Ducky used one like that when he played and choked way up on it. So he gave me this thick-handled bat and said, "Choke up and put the ball in play."

That was his great advice.

I was thinking, "Hey, if I could hit, I could have used *my* bat and put the ball in play."

I was 18 years old then, so I didn't say anything.

But it just goes to show you just how imaginative coaching can be at the minor-league level.

WELCOME TO PRO BALL

I had signed out of high school in Sacramento, and right away I flew out of San Francisco at 11:30 at night for rookie ball.

I took the red eye to Tampa and took a van—which my scout had called a "limousine" before I left—down to Sarasota.

I got to the team hotel at about 8 A.M., and I was ready to check in and get some sleep, and they said, "You have to report to the field at 10 A.M."

Remember, I was 18. I had sort of thought I was going to Florida on a vacation to play baseball.

And so I went to the minor-league complex and they gave me a uniform. It was wool. And it had patches in the seat from where other guys had ripped it up while they were sliding.

They didn't have enough caps, because there were too many players. So I got a batting helmet and put that on.

Eventually they started playing a game, and they put me in right field. I'd never played right field in my life. I'd never been picked last and had to play out there.

This was rookie ball, not spring training, so it was July 3 or 4 in Florida. And I was in a wool uniform.

What I didn't know was that every afternoon in Florida, it rains.

Those wool uniforms don't do well in the rain. Stink? Oh, yeah. And this was a clean one. I was standing out there in the rain thinking, "What am I doing here?"

And 21 years later, in my last year in the big leagues, I was still thinking that.

I'd be backing up third base and thinking, "What am I doing here?"

KING GEORGE

The first time I met George Kissell, the Cardinals' roving minor-league instructor, I had just gotten to rookie ball in Sarasota.

And I mean I had just gotten there.

In the morning of my first day, I was in that "B" game, I guess you'd call it. I don't know what it was, really.

But when that game was over, about 3:30 in the afternoon, I got back to the hotel and they said, "Report back at five o'clock for the night game."

I hadn't slept in almost two days, coming in from Sacramento, so I went up to my room and I overslept. I woke up at a quarter to five, and I just jumped in a cab.

I got to the complex where we played the day games, and I just gathered up my baseball stuff and ran to the bus. It was leaving right at five for the ballpark where we played the big night games.

And Ray Hathaway, the manager, came up to me when I was getting on the bus. And the only thing he said to me was, "Don't ever be late."

That was it.

So we got to the ballpark and the game started. There were rain delays, and I wasn't even playing, and I basically hadn't slept for two days.

There was this huge light pole in the middle of the dugout, and I was kind of sitting behind it.

This guy came and walked right in front of me and said, "What's the count and how many outs are there?"

Now, I didn't know George Kissell then. He wasn't the manager. I knew who the manager was. But figured I better find out the answers he wanted.

I leaned around the pole and looked at the scoreboard and read him the stuff he asked me about. I was thinking, "This guy can't even see the scoreboard."

He said to me, "Don't ever be on the bench and not know the count and how many outs. You always have to be involved in the game. If you're gonna sit there, learn something!"

I'd only been here a day, and I was thinking, "You've got to be kidding me. I don't even want to be here."

But now I know he was right. That's the bad part about it. I found out George was always right!

A JOLT FROM JOE

In 1969, I was the third baseman in Modesto, California, which was a Cardinals farm team in Class A ball. Al Hrabosky was pitching in Modesto when I was there. It was the best "A" team the Cardinals had. Joe Cunningham was the manager. He had me hit a lot of batting practice. Hey, just keep practicing your bad habits, and you'll reach not just "A" ball, but *the* highest "A" ball the Cardinals have.

After practice one day, Joe offered me the following piece of managerial wisdom: "Neither of us is going any further!"

Not long afterward, he was promoted to the team's front office, and I was switched into pitching.

Joe went on to have a successful career in group ticket sales for the Cardinals, and I played 16 years in the big leagues.

Joe had been right that day after batting practice: we hadn't yet found our niche.

A STRONG HINT

I was in the minor-league spring training camp in about '71 or '72. I was still playing infield and not doing well.

Bob Kennedy was the farm director then for the Cardinals.

We were at our complex in St. Petersburg, and one day he took me out to the garage where they kept the tractors that mowed the field and all that stuff the ground crew used.

Bob pulled up this garage door and brought out a push broom, one of those really big ones with the thick bristles and a handle that's like five feet long.

Bob was really strong. I mean, *really* strong.

He stood the broom on end, with the bristles on the floor, and he held the handle with one hand. Then he started lifting it gradually until he was holding it straight out away from him.

It looks like it should be real easy to do. It's just a broom, right? Try it, though.

That's what he had me do. I was six-foot-three and 170, 175 pounds. So I tried it, and I couldn't lift it an inch. Hey, I couldn't even have swept the floor with it.

Bob just looked at me and said, "That's your problem. You're not strong enough."

Right after that, they decided to make me a pitcher.

SWEET LOU

When you were a rookie, you didn't talk to anybody. And nobody talked to you. Not a veteran, anyway.

Whenever there'd be a road trip in spring training, I had to go every time as a backup pitcher. Just in case they ran out of real pitchers.

So I'd get on the bus and sit there and not talk for an hour or so till we got to the other team's ballpark.

But the thing about Lou Brock was, when he'd get on the bus he'd always sit right next to a rookie or a non-roster player. It was incredible.

Most of the veterans never even had to go on road trips in spring training. But Lou would go, and he'd sit down next to you and talk to you the whole trip.

It was just small talk, just to make you feel comfortable: "Where'd you grow up? Where'd you play last year? How'd you do last year?"

I was so impressed with that. That was Lou Brock.

He was always class. Absolutely.

COOL LOU

The most amazing thing I thought Lou Brock ever did was how he handled the stolen base record thing.

In '74, when I came up to the Cardinals, he was going for Maury Wills's season record of 104.

And he had death threats. He and Bake McBride both had death threats. Bake got them because he was going for Rookie of the Year.

The last month of the season, Lou had a guard with him all the time.

I remember one time, we were checking into the Hilton Hotel in Pittsburgh at 1:00 or 2:00 A.M. You check in and you get a little envelope with your room key in it.

Sonny Siebert got his envelope and they had his name written on it, but they had Brock's name crossed off. For some reason, they put Lou in a different room.

Sonny saw that and said, "I want a different room."

The hotel clerk asked him why.

And Sonny said, "If I go in that room and it's dark, people aren't going to know who they're shooting at."

It never seemed to bother Lou. He broke Wills's record with 118 stolen bases.

But late that season, we were playing in St. Louis, and I was sitting down at the end of the bench. And Bake came and sat down next to me.

I looked at him and said, "I'm sorry, Bake, but the guy might be a bad shot!" And I got up and walked away.

Poor Bake just sat there and looked at me like I'd killed his puppy.

Then I came back and sat down and started laughing. Bake didn't think that was too funny.

But he did win Rookie of the Year.

*Bake McBride... see, I told him I was just
kidding about avoiding him after his death threats.*

BASE BURGLARS

Base stealing, I think, is not so much speed as it is an explosive start.

Lou Brock had it. And Vince Coleman had it. The first couple of steps, those two guys just exploded.

Lou was the first base runner who made base stealing a science, even more so than Maury Wills did.

During games, Lou would sit in the dugout with a stopwatch, timing pitchers. He wanted to know how long it took each one to release the ball to home plate.

And he knew how long it took him to run to second. He didn't care about the catcher. The only thing he needed to know about him was how good his arm was.

With Vince, I don't know how he did it. He wasn't scientific. I know he stole third base a lot more than Lou did.

Vince had the green light to steal from Whitey Herzog whenever he wanted, except when Whitey gave him the stop sign.

If Vince didn't see that stop sign, he could go. And he did.

PINCH RUNNER I

One time Lou Brock had a sprained ankle. Red Schoendienst was the manager, and he sent Lou up to pinch hit, and Lou got a base hit.

But first base was as far as he could go on that ankle. So Red put me in to pinch run for him. And I was just in awe.

But I didn't plan to do any stealing. I was anchoring first base. There was no way I was going to get picked off.

But from then on, I could brag that I pinch ran for Lou Brock.

PINCH RUNNER II

One time in '82, Whitey pinch ran me for Dane Iorg. Dane had hit a double, and I was thinking, "Oh, man, I don't want to do this."

But when the manager tells you to do something, you've gotta do it.

So I was running onto the field, and I was near shortstop, and Dane was still standing on second base, and Dane said, "What are you doing?"

I said, "Pinch running."

And he said, "No!"

I said, "Whitey sent me out."

I was almost to second now, and Dane said, "What, do I have a broken leg and nobody told me about it?"

So Dane finally went to the dugout. The next day, he got to the ballpark and he was still angry about it. He said to me, "Come on, let's go race."

I said, "What are we gonna race for? Whitey thinks I'm faster."

So, did I race Dane?

Heck, no... he would have beat me!

LAWLESS AND ORDER

Tommy Lawless is a great trivia answer, because he was traded for Pete Rose in '84.

Pete was with Montreal, and Cincinnati traded Tommy to bring Pete back to the Reds. Then we got Tommy from Montreal in '85 for Mickey Mahler.

Tommy Lawless... making a name for himself with his World Series home run trot.

In the '87 World Series with Minnesota, I was in the on-deck circle at Busch Stadium when Tommy hit that three-run homer that won Game 5.

He hit that ball off Frank Viola, then he flipped his bat and stared at it.

I started yelling, "Run! Run!" Because that ball was coming down faster than it was going out.

Tommy kept staring at it, and it just got over the wall, and then he finally started toward first.

The thing was, Reggie Jackson was broadcasting the series. Remember, we had lost Jack Clark and we had lost Terry Pendleton. With them hurt, Reggie had said that we had all no-name players.

And he had used Tommy Lawless as an example.

So after that game, we're up three games to two, and we go back to Minneapolis for the last two games.

When Reggie came into the clubhouse up there, some of us said to him, "Hey, here's a no-name player you ought to talk to!"

We pointed to Tommy Lawless.

And you know what? Reggie went right over to him and started talking to him about his home run.

Reggie heard me then in the clubhouse. When I was in the on-deck circle, I don't think Tommy heard me... but trust me, I was yelling!

SURF AND TURF

We had a day game on that artificial turf at Busch Stadium late in Lou Brock's career. His legs were older, and the heat really bothered him.

Somebody decided that if they watered down left field, it would be cooler for him.

When you looked out, it was the only wet patch on the whole field.

So Lou ran out there, the game started and after the first inning, he came in and grabbed the dugout phone. I don't know who Lou called, but Lou was saying, "Whose idea was that? It's like a sauna out there!"

It was always hot out there for a day game on that plastic grass. And now Lou was standing in the middle of a steam bath.

STRAWBERRY FIELDS

When Whitey managed me here, he always had me in "B" games in spring training, because "B" games never count on your earned run average in the spring training. Only your "A" games count.

My arm was old, and it took me a *loooong* time to get up to speed.

One day, we were playing a "B" game against the Mets in St. Pete at their complex, Payson Park. Veterans don't usually play in the "B" games, so I thought I'd be pitching against the barely-made-the-roster guys.

But the Mets were going on the road for their "A" game, so they left their veterans behind so that they didn't have to ride the bus.

This was Darryl Strawberry's first year with the Mets.

I didn't know who he was. I was pitching, and this skinny kid got up there, and I threw a fastball inside.

He swung and missed. I thought, "I'll go back in there again."

I threw another fastball inside, and he hit it. He hit this ball into dead center field.

They had these palm trees out there, mature palm trees, and this ball was still going up as it went over the trees.

After the inning was over, I came back to the dugout, and Ricky Horton was on his knees, bowing to me.

On his knees!

He said he'd never seen a ball go that far, that quick.

And you know what? I didn't think I had, either.

ATTA BOY!

When Ricky Horton first came up and pitched for us, we were in San Francisco.

The first pitch he threw was either a home run or down the third base line for a double. It kept going like that. He threw three pitches and they hit all three, all line drives.

Ricky finally got out of the inning—I think somebody hit a line drive right at one of our guys—and he came and sat between me and Bruce Sutter in the dugout.

I said, "Nice going! You're throwing strikes!"

Bruce heard that, and he just put his head down, trying not to laugh till the kid went back out.

But that was the nicest thing I could think to say... the veteran consoling the rookie.

Once Ricky got settled in, though, he was hard to hit. He didn't throw hard, but his ball moved a lot. He threw the ball from right by his shoulder, and it was hard to see.

And he had a great change-up. The arm speed was the same as his other pitches, and that's why it was so deceptive.

I'd hit against Ricky in batting practice, and I could never hit him. But, hey, I was a .120 lifetime hitter. His ball didn't have to do much to fool me.

GIBBY AND THE ROOKIE

The nicest thing Bob Gibson ever said to me was in 1974, my first season with St. Louis.

We were in Montreal the last three games of the season, and we were tied for first place with Pittsburgh.

I had the first game of the series, and I went in to take a pee before I went out to warm up. Gibson came in and stood at the urinal next to me and asked if I was nervous.

Here was a man who hadn't talked to me all year, and this is the question I got. Here was a man who had a 1.12 earned run average one season, and 20 wins a year for a zillion years, and he was asking me if I was nervous.

I thought, "He probably wants me to say no."

For some reason, I was honest and said yes.

Gibby said, "Good! I always pitch better when I'm nervous. There's a difference between being nervous and scared."

And then he left.

So I just zipped up my pants and walked away, thinking, "Ooooh, if he pitches well when he's nervous, I should be *real* good!"

I couldn't believe that he would ever have been nervous. But I thought if Bob Gibson said it, that was good enough for me.

And I went out and won that day.

Bob Gibson, what a great competitor. Watching him in the clubhouse the day he was ready to pitch, nobody even made eye contact with him.

I mean, nobody. Not if you were smart. That was his day, and he was ready to pitch, and nobody better get in his way.

And *he* was nervous?

FISH STORY

In '82, when Bruce Sutter was here, we'd get up an hour before sunrise and go fishing on the days I wasn't pitching.

Herb Fox, a friend of Whitey Herzog's, had a strip pit over in Illinois. It'd take about 45 minutes to get there, and we'd get there at sunup and fish.

We'd always get off the water at 9:00 A.M. Then I'd always end up cleaning the fish, and Bruce would put the boat away and put all the fishing stuff back in the car.

Whitey would fish there, too, and he'd usually come up right as we were leaving and he'd ask, "Did you catch anything?"

One day, Bruce and I came off the water with our fish, and for some reason, we changed jobs. Bruce was cleaning fish and I was cleaning up.

Whitey pulled up as usual, and he said, "Hey, Bruce, just leave the fish. I'll clean 'em and I'll bring 'em down to the stadium this afternoon."

I thought, "Hmmmm. Whitey never offered to do that before."

I told Bruce, "That's pretty good. Next time, same thing. You clean the fish and I'll clean up the stuff."

So the next time, same thing.

Bruce got a knife and started to clean the fish, and Whitey came up and said, "I'll do that for you, Bruce. You go ahead, and I'll clean 'em and bring 'em to the stadium."

Whitey never told me, and I never asked him, but I think I know what he was thinking.

He didn't care if I cut *my* fingers with that knife, but he didn't want his stopper to get hurt. Because he never offered to clean the fish when I was doing it.

But it was good. I never cleaned fish again, and we always had fillets back at the stadium.

MATHENY THE MASTER

When Mike Matheny cut his hand on a hunting knife before the 2000 playoffs, he was lucky it didn't end his career. It was a gift, and he was opening the box, and it was still in the sheath when it sliced the little finger on his throwing hand. He couldn't believe that happened when the blade was still in the sheath.

The Cardinals really missed him in the playoffs, when they lost to the Mets and missed a shot at the World Series. Nobody blocks the ball better than he does. His mechanics are unbelievable. And I can't believe how tough he is.

When he was still with Milwaukee, I was watching a game where he was at bat and somebody hit him in the face with a fastball. The ball hit past the ear flap and got him right on the jaw. I mean, right on the jaw.

His knees didn't even buckle. He just dropped his bat and started toward first base.

I had met him before that, because his wife, Kristin, is from St. Louis and they lived here in the off season.

After he was traded over here, I said, "Wasn't that you who got hit in the face in Milwaukee that time?"

He said, "Yeah."

I said, "Didn't it hurt?"

He said, "Yeah."

I said, "You made me proud. You didn't go down."

And he said, "I didn't want the pitcher to think he hurt me."

I heard that and I just thought, "WOW!"

DON'T KILL THE UMP

With technology the way it is, it would be easy to put an infrared beam on the plate and have it outline the strike zone when a guy takes his stance.

Then you'd know exactly what's a ball and what's a strike. You wouldn't need an umpire.

I hope it never happens.

Baseball is the only major sport that doesn't use instant replay during a game. Some people want to use it to help the umpires. I say no.

Players make errors. Umpires should be able to, too.

I think the umpires get blamed for too much. In the '85 World Series in Kansas City, I don't think that call at first base in Game 6 lost the game.

The replay showed that the ump, Don Denkinger, missed the call. But that call didn't even cost us a run.

That just put a guy at first base. Then the Royals hit a foul ball that probably should have been caught.

And even when we lost that game, we still could have come back in Game 7.

I just think controversy is good. A call might not always be right, but it gives you something to talk about for years to come.

WHITEY ON WINNING

In '82, we were at the end of the season, and we were playing the Mets in New York. I was with Whitey Herzog and his wife Mary Lou over at somebody's townhouse in Manhattan.

Whitey was talking to the guy who owned the townhouse, and I heard Whitey tell him:

"The way you build a ball club is, you get to the World Series. For the next three years, you're guaranteed a lot of people coming out to the ballpark. That's when you get rid of your older players and bring in younger players.

"Then the younger guys have three years to mature and learn from the veterans that are still there."

We went to the World Series in '82, '85 and '87. And after each one, we'd get rid of older guys like Gene Tenace and Jim Kaat and Steve Braun.

My problem was, I never knew when that axe was going to fall on me. The last month of the '88 season, they traded me to Houston.

And at least I understood why.

LOSE FASTER

When Whitey took over the ball club in '80, we weren't very good.

Whenever we played, it seemed like our hitters were stepping out of the batter's box after every pitch, and our pitchers were taking forever to get the signals and throw a pitch.

So we went to San Francisco for a series. This was at old Candlestick Park, where it was windy and cold all the time.

Before the first game, Whitey called a clubhouse meeting to go over how to play defense against their hitters, like he always did right at the beginning of a series.

And while he was standing up there, Whitey said, "Now you pitchers, get up on the mound and throw the ball. And you hitters, get in the box and hit.

Whitey Herzog... lost in thought.

"If we're going to lose, lose fast. Let's try playing in three hours and leave."

Everybody kind of looked at each other and snickered. But it was understandable to me.

Nobody wanted to be there anyhow. We may as well get out of there as fast as we could.

BIG SPENDER

I came up to the Cardinals in July of '74 from Tulsa, and I joined the ball club at the airport in St. Louis. They had just finished a day game, and we flew to Cincinnati.

We got into Cincinnati, and the bus was there to take the ballplayers from the airport to the hotel. But the luggage truck was late.

So we checked into the hotel. I went up to my room, and after a while I went down to the lobby, and the luggage truck had just come.

My suitcase was there along with everyone else's, so I just grabbed it and took it up on the elevator to my room.

I was walking with it down the hall to my room, and one of the room doors was open. Some of the older guys, like Tim McCarver and Joe Torre, were in there playing cards.

They saw me walking by with my suitcase, and they said, "What are you doing?"

I said, "Carrying my suitcase."

They said, "The bellman's supposed to bring it up, and you're supposed to tip him. They've got kids in college. Do you want their kids to have to drop out of college?"

I thought, "Man, two bucks will really make that much of a difference?"

But I was too scared to say anything. So I just took it and moved on. Just another dumb rookie mistake.

That was the last time I took my suitcase up at a hotel, though.

THE BIG TIME

On that first road trip to Cincinnati, Tim McCarver caught my first big-league game.

I think it was the second game of a doubleheader. I pitched pretty well against the Big Red Machine, but I lost.

Nervous? Oh, heck yeah!

I went out to warm up, and I don't think the bullpen catcher got to catch too many of those pitches. They were going over his head and all over the place. I was just trying to get them in the vicinity of the catcher.

Back then, the bullpen in Riverfront Stadium was alongside the foul line in the outfield. It wasn't closed in. The pitcher had his back to the outfield wall, so when you missed the catcher, the ball would go all the way down between the dugouts and ring around the wall behind home plate.

I think a couple throws ended up in a bag of balls down there in the dugout.

Red Schoendienst was the manager then, and all Red said before I went to the mound was, "Go out and do the best you can. No matter what happens, you'll get another chance."

That was good to hear. I didn't know Red well enough to think he'd lie to me!

It turned out that I got called up because somebody had a sore arm and went on the disabled list, so they probably had nobody else for those two or three starts.

But I went out and pitched the first inning, and I did fine. The second inning, I went out to take my warmup pitches, and I decided to take a look around and see how many people really were there. I knew the stadium was packed, but I was too scared to look before.

I walked behind the mound and looked up... and almost threw up. There were 50,000 people there, and I knew they weren't there to see me!

We had gone over the hitters before the game, how to pitch to each one. The Reds had Pete Rose, Joe Morgan, Johnny Bench, Tony Perez, George Foster, Ken Griffey Sr.

Cesar Geronimo was their center fielder, and he was real fast and a threat to steal. They told me, "Just don't walk him. Make him hit to get on."

He ended up hitting a double and scored a run and hit a solo home run. And I lost two to one... but, hey, I didn't walk him!

REFLEX ACTION

We were in spring training in '75, and they split the pitchers up into two groups. One group threw batting practice the first day, and the other group threw the next day.

Red Schoendienst was managing, and he came up with this great idea: to sharpen the pitchers' reflexes, we'd throw batting practice without a screen in front of the mound.

My group was the first day. And right away, Lynn McGlothen took a line drive off his side... Alan Foster got one off his shoulder... and I got one off my shin.

So we lost three of our five starting pitchers the first day. The second day, Red put the screen up.

Talk about fast reflexes.

Red Schoendienst... his Hall of Fame reflexes are still good.

THE REDHEAD

Red was really good as a manager. He just made the lineup card out and let you play. He was a lot like Whitey in that respect.

Red was better managing a veteran ball club, where everyone takes care of himself and he didn't have to babysit. He wasn't a disciplinarian.

But after '74, they turned the ball club over and went with a lot of us younger players.

There were a couple of reasons. First of all, we didn't win.

And second, free agency was starting, and Anheuser-Busch, which owned the team, didn't want to pay the higher salaries.

But they didn't just want to lose players to free agency without getting something back.

GUSSIE BUSCH

Near the very end of the '76 season, Mr. Busch came in before a game to talk to us. And it was weird.

After batting practice, they told us, "Come in and put your jerseys on and sit in front of your lockers."

We had never heard anything like that before. So we sat there, and finally Mr. Busch came in. He had these note cards, the big ones like David Letterman has, and started reading this speech to the team.

I figured we had to put our uniforms on because he didn't know who any of us were otherwise. But he didn't talk to any of us by name. He just read those note cards.

He had like five words on each card, and he was flipping through them. We weren't playing very well, and the gist of his story was, "Just finish ahead of the Mets."

I don't know why he wanted that. I never found out. But we did finish ahead of the Mets.

Luckily, in '82 he was still alive and we won the World Series for him. And we finished ahead of the Mets then, too.

STAND BY YOUR MAN

We were playing the Mets here in '85 at Busch Stadium. Some of the Mets' wives were here, because it was a big series near the end of the year.

After the game, the visiting wives were supposed to wait for their husbands on the concourse level at street level, near the main ticket area, while the Cardinals' wives waited down on the clubhouse level.

The Mets had beat us that night, and the security guard, for some reason, had let the Mets' wives down on the clubhouse level. They had these Mets pennants. They were all excited because they had won. They were really yukking it up. And they were down on our wives' level.

All of a sudden, one of the guards came into our clubhouse and said, "You guys better get out here. Your wives are going to get into a fight with the Mets' wives."

We all went out there, but by that time they had gotten the Mets' wives back up to their level.

Later on, when I was leaving the stadium after the incident with the Mets' wives, I got on the elevator to take it up to the third level so I could walk across to the garage.

And Ray Knight, the Mets' third baseman, was on the elevator with his wife Nancy Lopez, the Hall of Fame golfer.

Nancy didn't have a clue who I was. Ray did, of course. She was telling him, "Those Cardinals' wives were really rude to our wives. All we wanted to do was celebrate."

Ray looked over at me, and all he did was roll his eyes.

At that point, the elevator door opened. They walked one way and I walked the other way.

The point is, the wives took it as seriously as the players did. More so, really.

For us, when the game was over it was over. You moved on.

But the wives, when someone came onto their turf, laughing after we lost, that was like waving a red flag in front of a bull.

MINOR-LEAGUE NO-HITTER

I signed with the Cardinals as an infielder-outfielder-pitcher. I hit well in high school, and I pitched well in high school.

But Bill Sayles, the scout who signed me—he also signed Keith Hernandez and Ken Reitz out of the Bay Area—said, "I think you can make it as an infielder."

I did get two Silver Sluggers for being the best-hitting pitcher in the National League. I got my first one in '75, my first full year in the big leagues, when I hit .308.

That surprised some people. I mean, I wasn't a very good hitter in the minors when I was a third baseman.

But I had fun, if you can have fun hitting a buck-fifty. I didn't even hit that in 1970, my last year in the minors at third base. I played third for three teams, and I kept going backwards because I couldn't hit.

I started at Modesto in '70 and hit .149, and I struck out 21 times in 47 at-bats.

Then I went to Cedar Rapids and I wasn't there long either. I struck out 19 times in 34 at-bats. That's a good recipe for a low batting average, and I hit .088.

Then I went down to Lewiston, Idaho, which was really just high-level rookie ball. And I hit .133 in 18 games.

Why did I hit so much better in the big leagues? Better equipment!

Actually, in the minors, I struck out so much because I didn't know where the strike zone was.

In the big leagues, everybody's pitches were around the plate, so I hit better.

And, in the big leagues, it's a cardinal sin to walk the pitcher. So any time a pitcher fell behind in the count, you knew a fastball was coming.

So it was harder for me to hit in the in the minors.

Here's how bad it got in Cedar Rapids. We were playing Waterloo, Iowa. I was playing third base and hitting eighth in the lineup. Our pitcher was hitting ninth.

I struck out three times in a row, and the pitcher behind me struck out three times in a row.

I came up for my fourth at-bat and struck out again. Our pitcher came up and—I'm sorry!—I wanted him to strike out, too. But he put the ball in play. He was out, but at least he hit the ball once.

I felt bad, but I never thought about changing positions and becoming a pitcher. What I thought was, "Oh, I just had a bad night."

COMMUNICATION BREAKDOWN

My first year of rookie ball, I was in Sarasota playing third base. There was a runner on second base and it was a bunt situation.

If the guy bunts toward third, you have two choices: either go in and make the play, or stay back and let the pitcher field the ball.

So I went over to our pitcher and said, "You've got everything on the third base line." He just looked at me and nodded his head.

He threw the pitch and the guy bunted toward third. I stayed back and the pitcher didn't cover the line. Everybody was safe.

When the inning was over, I came into the dugout. And George Kissell jumped me and started yelling at me for not fielding the bunt.

I said, "Hey, I told the pitcher that he had the third base line."

George looked at me and said, "He doesn't speak English!"

I didn't know. Hey, I just got there!

Of all the ways to mess up in the field, I'd never heard that one before.

And that pitcher probably still hasn't heard it.

SILENT GEORGE

I loved George Hendrick. What a great guy, even if you couldn't always understand why he did the things he did, like not talking to the press.

*"Silent" George Hendrick... a great team
guy who wasn't silent around his teammates.*

And after we got the last out of the '82 World Series, George never did come back to the clubhouse to celebrate. He just ran off the field through the wagon gate in right field, went under the stands, took his uniform off, changed into his street clothes and left.

He had played great. He got a huge hit when we scored those runs to go ahead. I couldn't figure out why he never came back.

So the next day, I called him up and said, "Where were you?"

He said, "I just wanted you guys to enjoy it. I was listening to the celebration in my car while I was driving home."

That was just George.

He was a great teammate. He was just a really good team guy, and he understood how baseball should be played. He would hit behind the runners.

He was a really good outfielder with a strong arm, and it was accurate, too. A guy like Dave Parker had a strong arm, but it wasn't accurate.

The only thing George couldn't do was hit a knuckleball.

I don't think he played the first game of the playoffs against Atlanta because Phil Niekro pitched. George said, "If I hit against a knuckleballer, my swing's messed up for a week."

We were laughing about that once before when he hit against Niekro. I told George, "Just go up there and don't swing. Just stand there."

So he did, and the first three pitches were balls. The next pitch was a called strike. The next pitch, George swung and missed. That made it three and two. On the next pitch, George swung and missed.

He came back to the dugout, and I said, "George, you had him! All you had to do was not swing."

And George said, "I know. But I thought I could hit him."

THE HAPPY HUNGARIAN

When I played with Al Hrabosky in Modesto in '70, he wasn't the Mad Hungarian. He was just Al Hrabosky, trying to make it to the big leagues.

He threw hard, harder than anyone we had on our team. And he was a starter then. This was before they really had closers. Teams had basically one reliever.

And the one thing you didn't want to be in the minor leagues was a reliever. That meant you couldn't make it as a starter.

Al could hit pretty well, too. Then again, I was comparing him to a certain third baseman hitting .235. Everyone was a pretty good hitter compared to me.

By the time I got to the Cardinals five years later, Al was the Mad Hungarian. He would go behind the mound to psych himself up, and he would throw the ball into his glove and march up to the mound.

One time with the Cardinals, we were playing Houston. Al went behind the mound and threw the ball into his glove, the way he did, like he was mad.

And he missed the glove!

I think the next three or four guys hit ropes off him, because he lost his concentration.

Then he definitely was the Mad Hungarian.

JAPANESE TOURISTS

After the '79 season, I played on an All-Star team that went to Japan.

We had an American League team and a National League team. The thing was, I didn't consider myself an All-Star. I'd never been to the All-Star Game, and I didn't really know anybody on the trip.

One time, we were on the bus after a game somewhere in Japan, on the way back to Tokyo where we were staying. Somehow the hitters started talking about pitchers throwing at them.

Bill Madlock was with the Pirates then on that "We Are Family" team that won the '79 World Series. He stood up and pointed to me and said, "Forsch, you hit people all the time!"

Well, I did hit him when he was with the Cubs. He slid into second base and tore up Mike Tyson's knee. So the first game I pitched against them after that, I hit Madlock the first time he came up.

The thing is, I hit him twice that game. The second one was a curveball. It wasn't my fault—it just slipped, really!—and it wasn't going that hard. But it did go off his helmet, which he didn't like.

So here he was on a bus in Japan, standing up and pointing at me. And I was thinking, "Nothing good is going to happen from here out."

Then John Candelaria stood up. I knew that Candy was about six-foot-seven, but I didn't realize how tall he was until all of a sudden, he stood up on that bus. He and Madlock were teammates in Pittsburgh, and I thought, "Uh-oh."

But Candy just said, "Madlock, if you got hit, you deserved it!"

I was feeling real proud then to be a pitcher.

*Another sticky moment with Bill Madlock—no, I
did not deliberately burst his bubble—in a bubble
gum blowing contest before a Cards-Cubs game.*

CHICKEN FEATHERS

The last year that Red was managing us, '76, was when the San Diego Chicken was real big.

We were not drawing anyone at Busch Stadium. We set a bunch of attendance lows that season.

We had a kitty with "fine money," which players assessed each other for messing up on the field or in the clubhouse. Teddy Simmons and Lou Brock thought we ought to take all that money from our fines and fly in the San Diego Chicken.

Simmons had to figure out a way to ask Mr. Busch whether it would be okay to fly in Ted Giannoulas, which was the chicken's real name.

Simmons somehow got the okay. We didn't have a lot of money in the kitty, but at that time the Chicken didn't charge a lot. He was just a radio mascot then. This was before he really started making appearances all over the country.

So the Chicken was here for the whole weekend. I don't remember how many people we had, and I don't know if anybody in the ballpark came to see him.

But I know that *we* were laughing at him.

SNAKE BIT

When we got Joaquin Andujar from Houston, I called my brother Ken, who was pitching for the Astros.

You hear stuff about guys and you always want to check it out. I thought I'd get a pretty good scoop from my big brother.

And Ken told me, "You're going to love Joaquin. He's so much fun in the clubhouse. But at least twice a year, he's going to say, 'I no talk to the press no more. I no talk to you guys.'

"And before the day's over, he'll be having 'em corralled and talking like nothing ever happened."

And my brother was right. Joaquin was a lot of fun. Especially when we found out he hated snakes. Any kind of snakes.

During spring training, we always had this trunk where you put your valuables. The first thing you did when you came in from the parking lot was put your valuables in your own little box in the trunk and lock it.

Buddy Bates, our equipment manager, was a prankster. One time, he took a fishing pole and flipped the line over the girders in the clubhouse ceiling. He pulled the line down and stuck a rubber snake on the end of it.

Then he reeled the snake up to the girders, right over the trunk, and then hid off to the side with the fishing rod.

When Joaquin came in to put his valuables in the trunk, Buddy let the snake down. It hit Joaquin in the head and fell down on the trunk.

Joaquin started yelling. I don't know Spanish very well, but I don't think he was saying, "Have a nice day!"

Before we could figure out all those Spanish curse words, he had hot-footed it out of there.

THE GOLDEN BOY

Joaquin won a Gold Glove one year from Rawlings for being the best-fielding pitcher in the National League.

He was so proud of that.

And Ozzie Smith also won one. Ozzie always won one. So he told Joaquin that they were bringing the Gold Gloves in the next day and presenting them in the clubhouse.

Joaquin had no idea how this deal worked. It was his first Gold Glove, and he was just so excited.

Ozzie went out and got one of those little bitty gloves, those souvenir gloves that you get in the concession stands, and spray-painted it gold.

The next day, we were all in the clubhouse for the Gold Glove ceremony. Ozzie pulled this little bitty thing out and said, "Señor Jack"—that's what Ozzie always called Joaquin—"since this is the first time you've won, you have to start out with this one."

And then Joaquin said the same thing he always said when we pulled something like that on him:

"You no good! None of you no good!"

ONE FUN DOMINICAN

Joaquin's favorite line was to call himself One Tough Dominican. And he really was.

In Game 3 of the '82 World Series, he got a line drive back at him that hit off his leg. Dave LaPoint and somebody else went out and carried him off the field.

I don't know who Joaquin said it to, but his only comment was, "Tell my Mommy I'm okay!"

He got the win in that game. Then he came back and pitched the seventh game... and won it to clinch the world championship.

He was a gamer. He was always ready to pitch. He was always late for spring training—he always had visa problems every year—but he was always in shape when he got there.

He just had to make that grand entrance. He was so funny. Just accidentally.

You never knew what he was going to do.

Joaquin Andujar... one fun Dominican!

SNOW JOB

Joaquin Andujar is from the Dominican Republic. When he came to St. Louis from Houston he had never seen snow.

After he got here, it snowed on one of our first home games in April. It was a Sunday day game and it snowed in the morning.

They still had the artificial turf at Busch Stadium, and they had that automatic tarp to cover the infield. There wasn't that much snow on the outfield, but there was snow on the tarp and they couldn't retract it.

So they called the game off. And then it started snowing again.

We were all in the clubhouse and Joaquin came over to ask me a question. I don't know why he chose me—maybe because my brother Kenny was on the Astros with him—but he said, "How do you drive in the snow?"

I said, "First of all, you've got to drive kind of faster than you usually would. Then you've got to get right behind the car in front of you. If you start sliding, you'll bump into the car in front of you and that'll slow you down."

The guys were listening to me and they couldn't believe I said something like that. But they knew I wouldn't have let him drive off like that. So they kept a straight face and I kept a straight face.

Joaquin looked at me, and he looked at me, and he started laughing. All he said was, "You no good!"

SHATTERED DREAMS

I don't know what happened when Joaquin blew up in the seventh game of the '85 World Series.

John Tudor started that last game in Kansas City. When Joaquin came in to relieve, I was busy warming up out in the bullpen.

We were both starters and it wasn't our normal day to pitch. But, hey, in the seventh game of the World Series, every pitcher's available. You've got all winter to rest up.

All I know is that Joaquin went nuts out there, and Whitey got thrown out, too. I came in to pitch after Joaquin left, and after I got out of the inning, I went into the bathroom off the dugout to take a pee.

I looked at the toilet, and the porcelain was gone. What was left of the bowl had a Jack Clark bat stuck in it. And the sink was gone, too.

That's when I figured we'd had a pretty bad day.

I came into the clubhouse and said, "What happened?" Somebody said, "Everything just went crazy."

The guys told me that Tudor punched a fan when he came out. I thought they meant fan, as in person.

After the game, I came in and "Tute" was sitting there with his hand bandaged up. That's when I realized he had punched an electric fan, not a human one.

And that was the end of the World Series. It went up in flames.

It was tough to take, especially since we should have won Game 6—with or without the bad call by Don Denkinger at first base.

And then getting blown out in Game 7, there was a lot of frustration. But when I came into the clubhouse, I didn't break anything.

The toilet... the sink... the fan... there wasn't anything left to break. It was all taken care of.

ONE GONE DOMINICAN

I never got a chance to talk to Joaquin after that last game in the '85 Series.

When we got home, everybody scattered. One thing about the end of the season—any season—is that everybody takes off when that last out is made.

In the '70s, we were so bad that the guys had their cars packed and waiting in the runway under the stadium behind the wagon gate. When the game was over, they were gone.

It's pretty much like that every year. Everybody's just glad to get out of there. You've been together since spring training in February.

I felt the same way even though I lived here. My philosophy was: during the season the ball club picks your friends, but after the season you pick your own.

Even so, I was friends with a lot of teammates away from the clubhouse. And I still am.

But Anheuser-Busch, which owned the team in '85, didn't like it when Joaquin went nuts on national TV in that last game of the '85 Series.

When the season was over, the word came down to get rid of him. And he was gone, just like that.

IN THIS CORNER...

I was in the middle of a clubhouse fight once that I had nothing to do with. I thought it was funny... once it was over.

It was a Sunday home game in St. Louis, and I was the starting pitcher. I got knocked out in the fourth or fifth inning—that happened to me regularly, actually!—and it was real hot. And I was hot.

I was not in a good mood after just getting a butt-kicking out there. I went right into the clubhouse, got out of my uniform and hit the shower. I was in there awhile and was just getting out, when I hear this yelling just outside the shower room.

It was Keith Hernandez and Roger Freed. The game was still going on, and they were just screaming at each other.

I had no idea what went on out on the field, and I couldn't really hear what they were saying. Their voices were echoing into the shower room.

I couldn't tell who was saying what. But I heard one of them yell, "Don't ever show me up in the on-deck circle again!"

Now, I'd had a bad day myself, and I'd already showered, and I was walking out in nothing but my shower shoes. And there are Keith and Roger, ready to start throwing punches!

I grabbed Roger from behind and we ended up on the floor. Stan London, the team doctor, came out of nowhere and grabbed Keith from behind.

I had hold of Roger, and I was saying to myself, "Not only have I had a bad day and I'm knocked out of the game, but now I'm breaking up a fight, and I'm on the floor of the locker room—with only my shower shoes on!"

Finally, the fight broke up and I thought, "Just another bad day at the office."

And I still don't know who did what to which guy.

THE RAPPER

Roger Freed came to St. Louis after Vern Rapp took over as manager. They had been together in the minors, and Roger had set all kinds of home run records.

So Roger was one of Vern's favorite players, but Vern wasn't too popular with many of the players. Vern knew baseball. He just wasn't a very good people person.

The first time I met Vern was before the 1977 season. We were leaving on the Cardinal Caravan, where guys from the team go meet the fans in the off season.

You ride a bus, and you go to communities all over the Midwest, not just St. Louis. We went to Iowa, Illinois, Tennessee, Arkansas and all through Missouri.

Vern was hired after the '76 season and none of us had met him. The day that the trip was supposed to start, a Monday, we got a blizzard and got snowed in. The Caravan couldn't leave St. Louis.

Our bus was scheduled to go out the next day, Tuesday morning, at nine o'clock from Busch Stadium.

I was picking up Pete Falcone and Eric Rasmussen, who lived here in town. We should have had plenty of time to get downtown. But the roads were still bad from the blizzard the day before, and it was morning rush hour, and the traffic was just awful.

We ended up being 20 minutes late to Busch Stadium. The other two guys took my suitcase to the bus with them while I parked the car.

Vern was sitting in the front seat of the bus, where the manager always sits. When I finally got on the bus, I said to Vern, "I'm sorry, the traffic was horrible."

His response was, "Don't ever be late during the season."

Which was a familiar phrase from managers.

My response to that was, "Vern, I don't think it's going to snow during the season."

Vern didn't think that was funny. He didn't smile or say anything. He just sat there.

And I thought, "Uh-oh, we're going to have a communication problem."

And we did. Everybody did with Vern.

UNIFORM JUSTICE

Before Vern Rapp came to St. Louis to manage, he had managed forever in the Reds' minor-league system. And the Reds were the strictest organization in baseball.

On his first day of spring training in '77, Vern told us he had a strict uniform dress code.

Sonny Ruberto was Vern's first base coach. But Sonny's job that first day of spring training was to stand on one of the steamer trunks in the clubhouse, like a model, so we could see how the Cardinal uniform was to be worn.

Vern said, "This is the way it's going to be."

* Socks showing the Cardinal stripes. No high stirrups, like all the players wore then.

* Neatly trimmed haircuts.

* No facial hair.

Vern Rapp's rule against facial hair is where Al Hrabosky and Bake McBride got into trouble. Al had a Fu Manchu moustache and Bake had real long sideburns. I guess we were supposed to play better if we looked better. But moustaches didn't hurt the Oakland A's a few years earlier when they won three straight World Series. And they did it against the Reds, who looked like we were supposed to look.

But Mr. Busch—Gussie Busch, our owner—backed Vern and all these rules. If somebody violated a rule, Vern wouldn't let the guy out of the clubhouse until it was taken care of.

So Al had to shave off his Fu Manchu. It was a little like Samson cutting off his hair. Al wasn't as effective when he lost his mean look. He wasn't the Mad Hungarian anymore. He was a choirboy.

Bake didn't want to shave his long sideburns. So Bake wound up in Philadelphia, wore his sideburns and eventually won a world championship with the Phillies.

We didn't play real well that season. We were two games over .500. But at least we looked good!

TRADE BAIT?

I didn't have a contract after the '76 season. Bing Devine was our general manager then, and Vern Rapp was taking over as manager. We couldn't come to terms on a contract in the off season. I went to spring training in '77 and just figured we'd work it out.

I wanted a three-year contract and X amount of money. But during spring training, Bing called me into his office and told me, "We don't want to give you that much money, and we don't want to give you three years."

And then he said, "Thank you. You've been a good Cardinal. And we're in the process of making a deal with San Francisco to send you there for Jim Barr."

So I left. I figured, "If they're talking, within a couple of days I'm gone."

I always liked Jim Barr. He was a really good pitcher, a stand-up guy you'd want in your rotation. He ate up a lot of innings for you. I'd have been proud to get traded for him.

In the meantime, I talked to my agent, who also represented... Jim Barr!

When I talked to my agent, I found out that Jim Barr was asking for a three-year contract... for almost twice what I was asking for.

A couple of days later, I was out in the batting cages at Al Lang Field in St. Pete, before the exhibition game that day. I was in my uniform, bunting and going through drills like that.

And Jim Toomey, our public relations guy, came out and told me, "Bing wants to see you in his office."

I thought, "That's it. The trade is done."

I figured, "If I'm gone, I'll be leaving before the team gets in from the game, and I'll never get to see everyone before I go."

So on the way in, I sort of said goodbye to everyone.

I finally got to Bing's office. And he said, "We've decided not to make the trade... because you've got too much potential."

Little did he know that I knew I had twice as much potential as Jim Barr—because he wanted twice as much money as I did!

Within a day or two, I signed a three-year contract for the money I wanted originally.

And that was the year I won 20 games for the first and only time in my career.

After I won that 20th game, I did a bunch of interviews afterward. I made a statement saying, "I'm really glad the Cardinals didn't trade me during spring training."

The next day we were on the field for batting practice. I was picking up balls and putting them in the bag for the batting practice pitcher, and Vern Rapp came up to me.

He says, "I read the article in the paper. And I want you to know we had no intention of trading you."

I just looked at him and laughed. I mean, how could Vern not know? Bing had me in his office for a reason.

And I said to myself, "There are communication problems all over the place here!"

To this day, I don't know if Vern knew what really almost happened with me.

And who knows how many other times I was almost traded?

BIG BROTHER

My brother Kenny is three and half years older than I am. He got to the majors as a pitcher before I did.

He was never part of a World Series winner, like I was in '82... until the fall of 2002. He was the assistant general manager for the Anaheim Angels. He had been out of baseball for a few years, selling real estate, when Whitey Herzog hired him.

After Whitey left the Cardinals, he became the Angels' general manager, and he put a lot of that World Series team together. And when Whitey was with the Angels, he hired Kenny.

So my brother went from selling real estate to getting hired as the Angels' farm director to being assistant GM of the world champions.

My brother and I never started a game against each other. Actually, we were scheduled to square off once in '82.

Kenny was with the Angels, and they were playing the Milwaukee Brewers in the playoffs. It was a best-of-five series, and he was scheduled to pitch the fifth game.

Gene Mauch was managing the Angels then, and he brought back somebody else on shorter rest to start the fifth game.

Because Kenny didn't pitch that game, he was scheduled to pitch the opener in the World Series.

I was scheduled to start Game 1 for the Cardinals. But Milwaukee won the fifth game, and Kenny never got to the World Series.

BROTHER VS. BROTHER

I did get to bat against my brother Kenny once in the big leagues.

I don't remember exactly when, but it was in the '70s in St. Louis. He was with Houston and he was their closer then. And he was good. He threw hard.

He made the All-Star team in the National League as a reliever with the Astros, and he made the All-Star team in the American League as a starter with the Angels.

When he was the closer in Houston, he usually only came in when they had a lead. I was a starter. So if I had a lead late in the game, they wouldn't be using him. And if they had a lead, it meant I was usually out of the game before he came in.

That's why we never faced each other. Except this one time.

We were ahead, but he hadn't pitched in a while and just needed some work that day.

And I hit off of him. I say I hit off of him, but I don't say I got a hit off of him.

There was a runner on third base and I think there were two outs. I hit what I thought was a sizzling ground ball to the shortstop, and he threw the ball away at first base.

So I was safe—on an error—and the run scored.

I don't know how many pitches Kenny threw me when I was up there. That part was a fog. All I know is that I put the ball in play. I didn't want to strike out.

I was just so glad I hit the ball... and that my brother didn't hit me first.

BROTHERLY LOVE

I want to say right here that my brother Kenny did a lot of mean things to me. Like when I got called up to the big leagues in '74. He was in Houston. I was with the Cardinals, and Bob Gibson is still there.

Gibby had this competitiveness where you did not talk to people on the other team before a game. Ever. For any reason.

If you did, Gibby fined you and the money went into the team kitty.

Plus, back then there was a league rule that you didn't fraternize with the other team. Players do it all the time now, and I hate that. It just looks bad.

Anyhow, Houston was playing us in St. Louis. The season was half over, and I hadn't seen my brother since the winter.

We were taking batting practice. I was out in left field shagging balls with the other pitchers when my brother walked out onto the field.

We shook hands and he congratulated me on making it to the big leagues. Then he left. That was it.

When batting practice was over, we left the field. Bob Gibson came over and told me, "That'll cost you 25 dollars. Don't talk to anyone on the other team."

This was my own flesh and blood! And Gibby obviously knew it. I mean, Kenny had his uniform on with "FORSCH" on the back.

Nobody spoke up and defended me. Hey, I was a rookie. And who's going to go against Bob Gibson?

You could appeal to a kangaroo court that veterans set up. But the fine was doubled if you lost. And you never won. Nobody ever won.

The fine money went for team parties and stuff like that. But this was 1974. And 25 dollars was a lot of money. Especially to a rookie.

So I paid up. And then someone told me, "Hey, if you do it again, the fine's doubled."

So after the game, my brother and I went out to dinner. I said "Kenny, I got fined 25 dollars for you talking to me on the field."

He just laughed.

I said, "This is serious. That's a lot of money to me. And if you do it again, the fine's doubled."

Later that year, we were playing in Houston. The Astros took batting practice and then we came out to take ours.

I waited until all their guys were off the field before I went out to shag balls with our other pitchers.

I was out in right field, and I saw Kenny coming out of their dugout on the first base side. He had his uniform on with "FORSCH" on the back and he was walking right at me.

I thought, "He knows I'll get fined 50 bucks this time and he's setting me up."

So when I saw him walking out toward right field, I immediately started walking over toward left field. I was walking over at the same speed he was walking out.

He kept coming and I kept going. Eventually, I ran out of room—hey, the outfield isn't endless—so I stopped. He came right up next to me.

I was a captive audience. But he didn't shake hands. He didn't say anything. He just stood there.

I said, "Kenny, this is costing me 50 dollars."

He just laughed. Then he turned around and walked away.

Of course, I got fined again—50 bucks, not 25. And I didn't try to explain this time, either. It was easier to pay the money than to argue with Mr. Gibson.

I still think about that after all these years. My brother never did pay me back.

I figure he owes me 75 bucks... plus interest.

MY BROTHER'S KEEPER?

Bob Gibson's whole idea of pitching was simple: When that hitter comes up to the plate, he can't be your friend. Or your brother.

When my brother Kenny pitched against us, he came inside with his pitches. A lot.

And he threw hard. Real hard.

Guys on our team would look at me like, "He's *your* brother... *do* something!"

I would sit there thinking, "Hey, if you don't like him... *you* go get him!"

How somebody pitches is how somebody pitches. There's nothing I can do about that. That's between you and him. But it is hard sitting in the dugout, watching your brother pitch against your team.

You want your brother to do well. But you don't want to lose.

ALL-STATE IS NO INSURANCE

When I signed with the Cardinals out of Hiram Johnson High School, I was probably one of the best seniors in the Sacramento area.

I was thinking of going to college at Oregon State, like my brother did. I had a full scholarship offer there and a half-scholarship from Southern Cal.

I was good for a high-school player in a town of 250,000 people. I made All-City, but I wasn't All-State or anything like that. I wasn't even All-Northern California.

Then I signed with the Cardinals. And when I reached rookie ball in Sarasota, Florida, it seemed like everybody there was All-State somewhere. I didn't realize then how many people lived in California.

You might not be All-State and still be pretty good. But I didn't realize that.

I got so intimidated in rookie ball with all these All-State guys. You sort of doubt yourself, whether you can compete with these people.

It doesn't help your confidence, especially when you find out everybody there was drafted ahead of you. *A lot* ahead of you!

I was selected in the 38th round of the amateur draft by the Cardinals.

That's bad enough, but as the draft went on, there were a lot of teams that took byes. A lot of teams were done drafting long before I got taken, because they thought there were no prospects left.

I didn't think about that at the time, so it didn't bother me where I got taken. Until I got to rookie ball and found out where I stood.

And after you make it to the big leagues, and you look back, you know that there were people who had more talent. But they were eliminated because they got hurt, or they didn't come in at night, or just didn't stick with it.

Looking back, you realize it's not always who has the most talent. Or who made All-State.

OWLS AND EAGLES

George Kissell, the roving minor-league instructor for the Cardinals, has a lot of lines that make a lot of sense.

One that he always told a young player was, "You can't hoot with the owls and soar with the eagles."

Translation: you can't be up all night and play well the next day. That will catch up to you no matter how much talent you have.

George would always talk about owls and eagles, and I knew he was right. Again.

I thought about those owls and eagles one time when we were in Philadelphia on a Saturday night. I was scheduled to start a day game there on Sunday.

I always got to sleep as soon as I got back to the hotel after a night game if I was pitching the next afternoon. I'd go to sleep at 11:00 P.M. or midnight at the latest, and then I'd always try to get up between 6:30 and 7:00 A.M.

Then I'd always go down and have breakfast, because I wanted my body to be awake for a one o'clock game.

This night in Philly, my hotel room abutted the room of a prominent player. I won't say his name. Let's just say he came to us late in the downward spiral of his career.

And this particular night, this player was having an all-night party next door to my room. My door was closed, obviously, so I couldn't tell who was coming in and going out. But it was non-stop traffic. The music was so loud that maybe I got two hours' sleep all night.

It was awful. But I still have to do my routine, so I got up at 6:00 A.M. and went down and got some juice and breakfast.

For the life of me, I don't know how I did it, but I went out and pitched well that day. I just always pitched well in Philly. I didn't always win, but I always felt comfortable in that ballpark, Veterans Stadium.

After the game, I went to the traveling secretary and requested never to room next door to this guy again.

I started to explain and the traveling secretary just laughed. He said, "You're not the first. We're running out of places to put him."

TAKE ME TO THE BALLGAME

The only big-league game I ever went to when I was little was in 1963, Stan Musial's last year.

My cousin Ernie Ehnisz was a Cardinals fan. He lived in Sacramento, but he loved Stan Musial. I was 13, and I was a Giants fan. Ernie was a grownup then, and he had four tickets to a game when the Cardinals made their last trip of the season to San Francisco.

Ernie and his father and my brother Kenny went to the game, and they took me, too. The only thing I remember from the game itself was that Willie Mays played for the Giants.

But what I remember most out of everything was that before the game, in batting practice, Stan Musial was fielding balls out in right field. And he was taking balls and throwing them over the fence to the kids in right field.

I was so envious of those kids. Our seats were better—we were right over the third base dugout—but I would rather have been in right field to get a chance to touch a big-league baseball.

Especially one thrown out there by Stan Musial. Oh, my gosh... and it wasn't even his home park!

Stan was all class back then in '63. And he still is today.

SAYING GOODBYE

My mom, Freda, passed away in 1980, the year Houston played Philadelphia in the National League playoffs.

My mom was very ill that season. My brother Kenny was tied up in the playoff race with Houston. I was the only one of us who could visit her in the hospital.

Whitey Herzog had just taken over as manager in St. Louis, and this is how good Whitey is.

He'd let me fly home to Sacramento between starts and tend to my mom and my dad, Herb, who was obviously having a rough time.

I would pitch a game, and then I would fly home for three days between starts, and then I would fly back and meet the team wherever they went next. I'd pitch again and then fly home again for three days.

The Cardinals weren't in contention, or I wouldn't have left the team. That's why my brother wasn't there at the hospital, even though he wanted to be.

But I don't know how many managers would let a pitcher take off like I did. That's how good Whitey is—not just as a manager, but as a person.

RED HOT

When Red Schoendienst managed here in the early '70s, it was the advent of hair dryers for guys.

We were in Chicago my rookie year, and the clubhouse in Wrigley Field was so old that it still had one of those radiator heaters in the bathroom.

In all the other ballparks in the National League, the manager had a separate bathroom. But Wrigley Field is so old, there wasn't room for a separate shower for the manager. So Red was using the bathroom that the players used.

He got out of the shower and was combing his hair. Being from the old school, he was not drying his hair with a blower.

But the players were. It was all cramped in the bathroom. Somebody who was using a hair dryer, moving it all around, accidentally bumped Red... and bumped him into the radiator.

The radiator was hot. I mean, it was *hot!* And Red had no clothes on. So when his rear end hit the radiator, he started yelling. I swear he had a horseshoe mark on his rear end.

Red was yelling, "Get those *bleeping* dryers out of here!"

That's when I knew a new generation had arrived.

TUDOR MONARCHY

John Tudor came over from Pittsburgh in '85 and got off to a one-and-seven start.

"Tute" was an unbelievable competitor, but he was a little different. Maybe it was because he was from Boston. People up there act differently than people here in the Midwest. I don't know.

But Tute was the kind of guy, if you gave him a million dollars in cash and some of the bills were wrinkled, he'd be upset. It seemed like he was never happy—which I later found out not to be true.

When John Tudor got off to this horrible start with us, you could say that he was really not happy.

We were in San Diego, and Tute got his lunch handed to him. Again. This was one of the last games he lost in that one-and-seven start.

John Tudor... with his motion in synch, he was tough to beat.

Our jerseys back then were pullovers. They didn't have the buttons up the front that they used to have—and that they have now.

When Tute lost in San Diego, he went up to the clubhouse and grabbed his jersey by the neck and just pulled straight down... and ripped it right down the middle.

I saw Tute do this, and it was hilarious. But you don't laugh. You can't laugh. The guy cares about losing. But it was still funny.

Buddy Bates, our equipment man, saw all of this. Now he had to go find another jersey so Tute had something to wear the next game.

I said to Buddy, "You ought to just sew buttons on it and put it back in his locker. He just turned a pullover into a cardigan."

But Buddy was too good of a person to do that.

John Tudor was a lefty, and when he was with the Red Sox he won in Fenway Park, with that Green Monster so close in left field.

That's why Whitey Herzog wanted him so bad here. Whitey said, "This kid got right-handed batters out in Boston. If you can get right-handed hitters out there, you can get them out anywhere."

That's why it surprised us all when Tute got off to that bad start with us.

But not long after Tute tore his jersey in San Diego, he was talking to a college buddy of his. I think it was a catcher from college or something like that. And the guy said to Tute, "You're kicking your leg up too quick."

It had something to do with slowing down his delivery. Whatever the guy said, it worked.

Tute only lost one game the rest of the season and ended up 22 and eight. That was really something.

TUDORING THE DOCTOR

The Mets were our big rivals, and it seemed like John Tudor would hook up with Dwight Gooden every time we played a series with them.

Gooden—they called him Doctor K because of all his strikeouts—was just a kid then. He was on a 100-pitch count so he wouldn't hurt his arm by over-working it.

Gooden would be throwing 95-mph fastballs, and Tute would be throwing 75-mph change-ups. And the score would be nothing-nothing till the eighth or ninth inning.

Then Doc would run out of pitches. He'd hit 100 and have to come out of the game. And then we'd score off the bullpen and Tute would hold them.

It was just fun watching him pitch.

DUGOUT ETIQUETTE

There are certain things you do and don't do in the dugout.

If someone makes an out, you don't say anything. Everybody knows what his job is. You feel bad enough about striking out or giving up a home run.

You don't want to hear someone say, "Hey, the guy hit a good pitch."

Well, Bruce Sutter always used to say, "I've never given up a home run on a good pitch."

If the guy could hit it out, it doesn't matter where the pitch was or what it was. It wasn't a good pitch.

Either he was looking there, or you shouldn't have thrown it where he was swinging.

THE STOPPER

I liked Bruce Sutter. I mean, I really liked him. Every day that he came to the ballpark, you could count on him to pitch.

Whitey protected him. He never used Bruce more than three days in a row so his arm wouldn't get worn out. But if you needed Bruce on that fourth day in a row, he'd go do it.

Whitey would never do this, but if he gave the ball to Bruce and said, "Go pitch," Bruce wouldn't care how many days in a row he pitched.

I'd never been around a reliever with a better demeanor than Bruce Sutter.

When Al Hrabosky was our stopper, he was visibly ticked off if he missed a save... until he got the ball again in a save situation. It could be days between appearances, and Al would be ticked off the whole time.

With Bruce, when the game was over, you didn't know if he saved the game or lost the game. He had his own little cooler of beer in front of his locker, and he'd just sit there and have a couple of beers when the game was over.

But he didn't lose too many games.

RAIN OR SHINE

One time in Cincinnati, the Reds had the winning run on second base. Bruce Sutter took his warmup pitches, and all of a sudden, it started pouring rain.

They covered up the field and we had a rain delay. In Cincinnati, they didn't call games. It didn't matter how big or small the crowd was; they just didn't call games.

Bruce Sutter... the demeanor of a reliever.

So we had about an hour and a half rain delay. They finally took the tarp off, and Bruce went back out to warm up.

The batter stepped in, and on Bruce's first or second pitch, the guy hit a line drive into the gap. The run scored from second base and we lost the game.

We came into the clubhouse, and Bruce said, "Hell, if I'd have known that, I wouldn't have taken so many warmup throws before the rain delay, and we could have gotten it over with then."

Now *that's* the demeanor of a reliever. Bruce knew he would get the ball again in the next save situation we had.

And when he did, he knew he'd save *that* game.

RIDIN' HIGH

The best three relievers in baseball when I played were Bruce Sutter, Rollie Fingers and Goose Gossage.

Technically, we had Bruce and Rollie together on the Cardinals for a few hours before Whitey sent Rollie to Milwaukee. That was the trade that put both teams in the '82 World Series.

Bruce threw that split-finger fastball, and it would just drop straight down to the hitter. But he'd blow a fastball past you, too.

The last pitch of the '82 World Series was a fastball. Bruce blew one by Gorman Thomas after Gorman had fouled off a bunch of split-fingers.

It was a rising fastball, and that's how we finally beat the Brewers. Bruce called it a "high rider." He thought it was somewhere in the 90-mph range, but I'm thinking it was somewhere in the middle 80s.

It just seemed harder to the hitter after all those split-fingers dropping in there.

GONE FISHIN'

Bruce and I had a lot of fun when he was here.

In spring training in Florida, we used to fish off the sea walls in St. Pete. We'd use live shrimp for bait, and we'd fish for sea trout.

We all had rental cars during spring training because we would all fly down to Florida. So when Bruce and I went fishing this time, we took his rental car back to where we were staying.

Bruce had the remainder of the shrimp in a bucket on the floor of the back seat. Somehow the bucket spilled while we were driving. And we didn't notice that the shrimp were lying on the floor back there.

Bruce went back to where he was staying and parked the car. It just sat there, with the windows rolled up and the shrimp all over the floor, for about four days, with the temperature in the 80-degree range.

This was near the end of training camp. It was time for the club to leave and go back north, so Bruce had to take the car back to the rental place.

When he opened the door, it smelled so bad back there from all the dead shrimp. I mean, he said it smelled *bad!*

I asked him what he did. And Bruce said, "I just got in, rolled the windows down, drove to the rental place, dropped the keys off and left."

There it is again... the demeanor of a reliever.

But he did at least take the shrimp out of the car before he dropped it off and ran!

TEMPER, TEMPER

I never saw Bruce Sutter lose his temper. Never. He never changed, whether he won or lost.

The only times I ever remember him saying anything were when reporters questioned him after he didn't get a save.

Bruce would say, "Hey, if you don't come up and ask me about every save, don't come up and question me when I don't save one."

That seemed fair to me.

ASK A STUPID QUESTION

I grew up in Sacramento, and the Giants were the closest team to us. So when I was with the Cardinals and we came to San Francisco, sports writers would come over from Sacramento to cover the games.

This one reporter came over once when I pitched at Candlestick Park... and this might have been the angriest I ever was at a sports writer in my life.

I was pitching a shutout, or we were tied at one, or something like that. And in the bottom of the ninth or 10th inning, Mike Ivie hit a ball down the left field line that curves around the foul pole. It's fair. It's a home run. And we lose.

When you lose in the bottom of the last inning and have to walk off the field, that's disheartening. You're the Maytag repairman. You're the loneliest man in the world.

That's a long walk. I mean, that's a tremendously long walk on any field.

But at Candlestick Park, you had to walk all the way down the right field line to get to the clubhouse. It wasn't attached to the dugout.

So I finally get to the clubhouse after this *loooong* walk. And the sports writers are waiting for me. I knew the St. Louis writers really well, Neal Russo and Rick Hummell from the *Post-Dispatch* and Jack Herman from the *Globe-Democrat*.

When you travel with writers, they know your demeanor. They know what to ask, and how to ask it, and when to ask it, and what not to ask. Usually after a home run like that, they want to know what pitch was hit—the mundane question they always have to ask.

But this time, this jerk from Sacramento says to me, "I guess since you grew up as a Giant fan, this loss isn't as hard to take."

And I say, "That's the most stupid question I've ever been asked. I don't play for the Giants. I play for the Cardinals."

I'm barely looking up, and I'm getting hotter. I say, "This interview is over. Get away from me... *now!*"

To the credit of the St. Louis writers, they left also. And then after I showered and cooled off, they came back and we finished the interview.

But I can't believe anyone would ask a question like that. I know it's only a game, but it's winning and losing.

And I wouldn't care if I'd been playing a Little League game. It hurts to lose.

POISON PENS

Some writers could really be nasty.

Bobby Sykes was a left-hander we traded to the Yankees for Willie McGee, which was a great trade for us.

When he was here, Sykesie was struggling. He was pitching his butt off, but he was struggling.

And some guy wrote something about him like, "Sometimes you lead the elephant, and sometimes you walk behind the elephant and sweep up."

It was cruel. It was really cruel. Sykesie was trying. You don't go out there and try not to win games.

I think sometimes writers and fans forget that.

TLC, PLEASE

I talked to Whitey Herzog once about handling players, and he said something I never forgot.

He said, "I don't need to talk to the eight guys who are out there every day. They know how they're doing. They're in the lineup. They can read about themselves in the paper.

"I need to talk to that 23rd or 24th or 25th man on the ball club. They've got to feel like they're a part of the team. It's a long season, and I'm going to need those guys on the end of the bench. They're going to end up helping us win."

So during batting practice, he'd go out and talk to the guys who weren't playing as much.

And Whitey was right.

In '82, Ozzie Smith got hurt. And Mike Ramsey stepped in at shortstop for him and just played solid baseball.

We *were* defense. That's how we won. Mike stepped in and we never missed a beat. Then Ozzie came back, and we went on to win the World Series.

JACK THE RIPPER

We got Jack Clark from San Francisco in '85, and boy was I glad.

He had a great arm. He played first base for us, but he played right field for San Francisco. The scary thing was, on hard-hit balls to right field he would try to throw the batter out at first base.

He did that a lot. And he got a lot of outs at first base that way. He'd catch a ball on one hop and come up throwing.

When we played the Giants, I remember getting a hit to right field and running as fast as I could so he wouldn't throw me out at first. I didn't want to be embarrassed.

He was the only right fielder in the league you had to worry about like that.

Mostly, I hated pitching against him. He could hit some shots. He'd cock that back foot when he was ready to swing. As a pitcher, you'd see him do that, and that was just a bad feeling.

You knew he was locked in.

When Clark came here, he told the papers that he had been on winning teams before in San Francisco, so he knew what a pennant race was.

Gene Gieselmann, our trainer, cut the quote out of the paper and showed it to me. We checked the stats, and we found out that their best finish was second or third when Jack was out there.

So we cut that out of the record book and put it in his locker, along with the quote. And we told him, "That's not a pennant race. Coming in second or third is *not* a pennant race."

Jack didn't say anything. He couldn't say anything. He was probably too embarrassed to get mad!

When we were ready to clinch in '85, Gene and I went over to Jack and asked him if he knew why all the plastic sheets were over everybody's lockers.

He just looked at us and said, "I can guess."

Jack Clark... whipping his bat into warp speed.

They put plastic sheets on the lockers to protect everybody's clothes and other items from the champagne that you spray when you celebrate.

We told Jack, "*That's* when you're in a pennant race."

And he just laughed.

Winning was a whole new thing for Jack. When he got here, he was funny, naïve, in a never-been-there-before way. He came from San Francisco, where it was cold and nobody came to the games and they never won. He was the star there, and he had the burden of the whole team on him.

Then he got play here in St. Louis, which is obviously the best place to play baseball—no question. The ballpark is packed and the fans are so knowledgeable and they appreciate good plays.

When Jack came here, he was a perfect fit. We had a lot of talent but we needed a power hitter.

And he was one of the few guys who could hit it out of Busch Stadium *before* they moved the fences in.

SPRAIN GAME

When Jack Clark hurt his ankle in the '87 season, that was the ugliest sprain I'd ever seen.

We were playing Montreal, and he was running to first base and tried to dodge Andres Galarraga, who had the ball and was waiting to tag him.

Some people thought Jack just should have let himself get tagged out, but I didn't have a problem with him trying to do what he did.

I know the fans and media wondered why an ankle sprain was taking so long to heal.

It was like a high ankle sprain, except they didn't call it that back then. His foot looked like an eggplant, all purple and swollen.

Everybody wanted him to come back and play in the postseason. And Jack did everything he could to get back out there. Gene Gieselmann did everything he could to get him back, too.

But the club never said how bad the sprain was. We didn't even really know for sure. He'd try to take batting practice—real early so the reporters wouldn't see—and you could tell he couldn't put any weight on his ankle.

The club just said, "He's not available." That way they could use him as a decoy. The other manager wouldn't know if Jack could pinch hit late in the game or not.

Jack was so important to our team. He was the only one who could hit a home run. He was the only chance we had. We could be down by three runs, and he was the only guy we had who could win the game with one swing.

Just ask Tommy Lasorda and the Dodgers. Jack hit that two-out, three-run homer in the ninth inning against Tom Niedenfuer in Los Angeles that put us in the '85 World Series.

THE CARDINAL WAY

We were in a spring training game once, and Andy Van Slyke was a young outfielder then. And Andy caught a fly ball the way Dave Parker used to—he snapped his glove down on top of the ball, real fancy, instead of just letting the ball fall into his glove.

I was a veteran then, but I was just a member of the team. It wasn't my ball club. But I went over to Andy and I said, "That's not the Cardinal way. Don't *ever* drop a ball doing that." Andy didn't say anything.

Late that same season at Wrigley Field, a fly ball went out to Andy in right field, and he slapped his glove down on it again... and the ball fell on the ground. And a run scored.

*Andy Van Slyke... he learned the hard
way that the Cardinal Way is not a snap.*

When Andy came in after the inning was over, nobody said anything to him about dropping that ball. Not even Whitey. Finally, I couldn't stand it any more. I went over and said, "Andy, outs are too hard to come by. They're too valuable. Just catch the ball."

Danny Cox was pitching that game. He was just a kid then, so he hadn't said anything to Andy, either.

But when Danny heard me, he came over and said, "Thank you."

And Willie McGee told me, "I'll never forget that."

That was the first game of a doubleheader. I don't remember if we won or lost. But I remember I found out later that Andy felt so bad, he didn't even go up to the clubhouse to eat anything between games.

I felt bad about that when Ricky Horton told me... about 10 years later. But that's not the Cardinal way to play baseball. That's the bottom line. It's all about winning. Andy understood that. That's why he stayed in the dugout between games. And Andy learned. He became a great player after we traded him to Pittsburgh—playing the Cardinal way.

NO REST FOR A WEARY TEDDY

The thing that really impressed me about Teddy Simmons was that he caught I don't know how many games in a row in the hot months, July and August.

One time, I was pitching a Sunday game after we had played a Saturday night game. On the way to the ballpark, Teddy said, "Boy, could I use a day off."

Red Schoendienst was the manager then, and I said, "Just go in and ask Red."

Teddy said, "No, I won't do that."

He never, ever asked for a day off. Never. He just wouldn't do it. And when he did get a day off from catching, he'd play left field or somewhere else. When we got to the park, I went in and told Red, "Teddy needs a day off. We rode in together and he's really tired."

Red said okay, that Teddy didn't have to catch.

But I was pitching, remember? So I said to Red, "Hey, if you need a pinch hitter today, he's available!"

Even if Teddy Simmons wouldn't ask for days off from catching, he appreciated it when he got them.

We had a Sunday day game in Cincinnati once and it was smoking hot. Just terrible.

Steve Swisher, our backup catcher, was playing and Teddy was in left field. Swisher's first time up, he hit a double or triple. And I thought, "Uh-oh."

First of all, he wasn't used to playing, because Teddy caught almost every game. Second, Swish wasn't used to playing in that heat. Third, he wasn't used to being on base. And fourth, he wasn't used to running past first base.

I was in the dugout watching Swish after that inning, and he was starting to wilt. I said to Teddy, "Swish won't make it through the whole game."

Teddy said, "He better." And Teddy wouldn't even walk down the dugout to see how Swish was doing.

We had only played a couple innings, and Gene Gieselmann was doing everything he could to keep Swish in the game.

He was already into the ammonia water. You splash it on your face and it evaporates fast and cools you off.

You could just see what was coming.

Swish was gone by the fifth inning, and the last time I saw him he was up on the training-room table... packed in cold towels.

And Teddy didn't say a word. He just trudged over and put on the catcher's gear.

HALL MATERIAL?

Teddy Simmons was my catcher, but we also became really good friends. We drove down to the ballpark together for every home game.

So I may be prejudiced, but I think Teddy's been slighted for the Hall of Fame. Without a doubt.

He was a switch hitter. If you look at his batting average— .285—not many catchers hit better than that. He didn't get leg hits, and we had nobody in the lineup to protect him. But, man, he could hit line drives.

Some people say his defense wasn't good, but I thought he had a bad rap.

He didn't have a strong arm, but he got rid of the ball quick. He pitched out a lot, but that didn't bother me because I had pretty good control. He could pitch out twice on a hitter with me, and I thought my control was still good enough to get the guy out.

And Teddy called a good game.

If hitters knew a catcher's tendencies, I sometimes think they could be better hitters. Because catchers call pitches they can't hit in certain situations. Teddy didn't do that, because he could rake. He could hit in any situation.

After we traded him to Milwaukee, I pitched against him in the World Series in '82 and gave up a home run to him. He hit a fastball.

I think he knew my tendencies, too!

Anyway, a reporter called me from New York and asked me if Gary Carter should be in the Hall of Fame. I said, "No way. Not unless Ted Simmons is in there first."

The guy said, "Look at Carter's batting average for a catcher."

I did. It was .262, with 324 home runs and 1,225 runs batted in.

And I said, "Look at Ted Simmons and what he hit as a catcher."

Celebrating my first no-hitter with
Teddy Simmons... a Hall of Famer in my book.

Teddy hit .285 with 248 home runs and 1,389 RBIs.

They said Simmons wasn't a great catcher, but when you tried to steal on Carter, the ball always fell out of his glove before he had to throw it.

In fact, both of them fielded .986 for their careers.

But... Gary Carter played in New York, with all the media coverage there. That makes a difference.

And they won a world championship while he was there. That makes a difference, too.

But not enough to make the Hall of Fame ahead of Teddy Simmons.

RUBBED WRONG

You know how some guys just bug you? Gary Carter bugged me... bad!

I was pitching in Montreal in '83, and it was not a good season for me. And I was not having a good ballgame, and I was giving up runs. And Gary came up.

You always had to pitch Gary inside so he couldn't get his arms out and pound the ball. So I was pitching inside, and I had three balls on him, and I threw a pitch that was sort of tight. It just ran in on him for ball four.

He went down to first base. And on the way he said something to me like, "Throw the ball over the plate."

I wasn't feeling real great. So I said, "The next one you get will hit you."

I ended up getting knocked out of that game before he came up again. We didn't see the Expos again until near the end of the season.

Everybody on my team knew that I was hitting Gary Carter on his first time up. Believe it or not, some of our guys came in before the game and told me, "His teammates said if you hit him, we'll back you."

I guess he wasn't too popular in his own clubhouse.

So the first time he came up, he was in the back of the batter's box. I don't know if he knew what was coming. All I know is, he stood a lot closer to the plate the last game I pitched against him.

I missed him with the first pitch, but I got him with the second pitch. Both fastballs.

He went to first base and didn't say a word. It was September 26, 1983. And I know that because that was the day I pitched my second no-hitter.

I hit Gary in the second inning, and the rest of the game just fell into place. And no, hitting him didn't ruin a perfect game. There was an error later on.

The following year, the first time we played the Expos, George Hendrick came into the clubhouse before the game and said:

"Hey, Gary Carter wants to talk to you outside on the runway."

I had no idea what he would want to talk to me about. So I went out there, and to his credit, Gary said, "I play hard. Every day."

And he did.

I told Gary, "I pitch hard. Every day."

And I did.

That was all. It was done. I respected him for coming up and saying that. And we never had a problem after that.

CHARTER MEMBERS

We flew charters almost all the time. When we flew on Ozark Airlines, they took care of us like you wouldn't believe. I thought they were a great airline.

But during the start of free agency, when Anheuser-Busch still owned the Cardinals, the brewery had the opinion that is still there today among some people—that we were too pampered.

This was when Vern Rapp was the manager and John Claiborne was the GM.

So they did away with the charters, and we started taking commercial flights. And then we started getting into all kinds of situations.

One time, we had a game here at home that was stopped and put on hold, because we had a commercial flight to catch. Which was unheard of then. And now.

So we went back to taking some charters. But things could still go wrong there.

One time we were in New York and had just finished a night game with the Mets. We were flying home after the game with an off day the next day.

The games at Shea Stadium started at eight o'clock then, New York time. So they got over late. When this game was over, we went to La Guardia Airport to catch an Ozark charter to go home.

We got to the plane about midnight, and everybody was on board, and we had a mechanical problem. Which meant we couldn't take off.

And since Ozark really didn't have gates there, or some deal like that, they pushed the plane out on the tarmac to fix it.

We were still on the plane, and it turned out there was no mechanic to fix it. So Ozark had to send a mechanic from St. Louis. At least that's the story we were told.

Meanwhile, I was looking out the window, and a guy with a rubber mallet was pounding underneath the wing. And there was fluid leaking out.

I didn't know what that was, but I was thinking, "We're going to be here awhile."

We sat there on the plane on the tarmac, and we ate everything and drank everything, and then it was about five o'clock in the morning. And the plane still wasn't fixed.

Finally, they told us to get off the plane. We took a bus over to Kennedy Airport and got on a different Ozark flight back to St. Louis.

We finally arrived home on our off day about 9:00 A.M. Then we found out that our other Ozark plane was only a half-hour behind us getting into St. Louis.

The day was just starting, but all you wanted to do was go home and go to sleep.

One off day totally shot.

DOWN TIME

When Whitey was here, if we had an off day at home, we didn't fly out till the next morning to go play a game that night.

He felt it was important to be with your family. Knowing Whitey, he was probably fishing that whole off day! But his point was, you get tired of looking at the same faces all the time.

Usually, when you have an off day on the road between series, you finish the first series and fly to the next city to have the off day there.

When you get there, you sit around the hotel room and watch television and then go out to dinner. Baseball players aren't much on sightseeing. I don't know why. All I know is, I didn't hear too many guys say, "Yeah, I went over to the Statue of Liberty," or "I went over to the Liberty Bell."

A lot of ballplayers would go out and play golf. I wasn't a golfer, and we didn't have a lot of golfers on the team then. The guys who did golf had to rent clubs on the road, because Whitey wouldn't let them bring their clubs on the trip. He thought it was a distraction.

But when Whitey was here, if there had been an off-day fishing tournament anywhere, I think we could have won it.

Whitey was the best at keeping fish and not throwing them back if they're too little.

The joke was: if it was big enough to hook, it was big enough for Whitey to keep.

But then he always gave the fish away to people—the coaches, the clubhouse guys, anyone around the clubhouse.

The thing is, he still does that today. He'll go on a fishing trip somewhere and come back with fish for all kinds of people.

THE SMART RAT

Everybody who worked around the ballpark liked Whitey so much. He knew baseball. He knew what he was talking about.

People don't realize this, but when the Angels won the World Series, Whitey had put a lot of the core of that team into place. When he was the general manager there, he had a lot of those guys coming up through the minors.

When he took that Angels GM job, I didn't realize that he never moved to Anaheim. He just ran the club over the phone from home in St. Louis.

The White Rat was the only guy I ever heard of who could run a team by long distance. But he had done just about everything you could do on a ball club. He played in the big leagues, he coached in the big leagues, and he was farm director for the Mets.

He knew the situation that people were in, and he took care of them.

THE CARETAKER

Butch Yatkeman, our old equipment man, was going to retire in '81, the strike-shortened year. He had been there forever and he was only making $8,000.

That's hard to believe. Whitey found out about it when he came over in '80. He was the manager but then he moved up to GM, and he got Butch a $20,000 raise.

That helped Butch's pension, too, because it was based on his salary.

Then Whitey told Butch, "Stick around just another year. I think we've got a pretty good team."

So Butch held off retiring until after the '82 season. We ended up winning the World Series, and he ended up with a full World Series share to boot.

That's what I mean about Whitey taking care of people.

HATS OFF

God bless Butch Yatkeman, but when he ran the clubhouse you got one cap at the beginning of the year. And that was it.

Now, they get all the caps they want. Butch gave us one cap, and it had to last all season. I mean, through those summer months in St. Louis, the sweatbands inside those caps would start to stink.

Now, they've got a guy like Steve Kline, who messes his cap up on purpose. He puts dirt on it and spit on it and who knows what else.

Why would you want to wear a cap that smells bad? That boggles my mind. Why would you want to put your head into something like that?

I don't know, maybe it doesn't smell as bad on the inside as it looks on the outside!

But I guess the good thing is, nobody's going to take your cap in the dugout. And it's always easy to find your own.

WORK PLACE

Whitey was different from most managers. He would not allow any food in the clubhouse.

He believed that you ought to get out of the clubhouse when the game was over and go home and eat with your family.

And we had no TVs in the clubhouse. He felt that you don't need to watch a game show before you played a baseball game. He wanted us thinking about baseball.

Now, the guys can watch a lot of TVs in the clubhouse. But they put on tapes of who's pitching against them that day, and tapes of the last time he pitched against the Cardinals.

They did that in Houston when I was there the last month of '88 and all of '89. That was the first time I saw that, using TVs to get ready for the game.

HOUSTON BOUND

I didn't like being traded after 15 years with the Cardinals.

But I was thinking about retiring, and getting out of baseball for a couple of years, and then getting back in. So I wanted to see what another organization was like.

Plus, I was near the end of my career in '88, and I could understand the Cardinals trading me.

Really, the hardest thing about getting traded was the way I was told. I had just pitched a game here in St. Louis and then we went to Atlanta.

Dal Maxvill, the general manager, called me on the phone about three o'clock in the afternoon. I was already at the ballpark and already in uniform.

As usual, there was nothing to do on the road. I'd rather get to the ballpark. There was always a card game or something going... you know, the fraternity, the road show.

And I get called to the phone in the clubhouse. And Dal said, "We've made a trade and you're going to Houston."

That was it.

Except I told him, "Hey, you can't trade me without my consent."

See, when the Cardinals told me they were trading me to Houston, I was a "10 and 5" player. I had 10 years in the big leagues, the last five with the same team.

And so I had to approve any trade.

That wasn't something in my contract. That was something in Major League Baseball's basic agreement with the Players' Association. It applied to every player who was 10 and 5.

Dal told me, "Well, if you stay here you're not going to pitch again."

When I heard that I was a little shocked, to say the least. I was still starting then and pitching well, really. I was nine and four.

So I didn't tell Maxvill then whether I'd go to Houston or not. I waited until Whitey came into the clubhouse and asked if I could talk to him.

He said, "Sure, come into my office."

I told him that Maxvill had said I was being traded. Whitey said, "Yeah, I know."

I told him that I was a 10-and-5 guy, and that I was thinking of vetoing the trade, but that Maxvill had told me I wouldn't pitch the rest of the year.

I said, "What is my situation here? Will I pitch?"

Whitey said, "It's my team. And nobody's telling me who I'll pitch and who I won't pitch."

Then I asked Whitey what my situation would be for the next year, the '89 season.

He said, "The same situation that it's been for the last three years."

Which meant I'd have to make the team in spring training. My contract was up after the season. I always had a one-year deal. I'd been year to year since '86.

Houston needed to know right away if I would agree to the trade.

This was in late August. You have to be on the team you're being traded to by midnight of August 31 or you're not qualified to play in the postseason.

The Astros were in first or second place in their division. So if I went there I might get a chance to pitch in the playoffs.

And Hal Lanier was the manager there. I knew Hal real well and really liked him.

He was on those Giants teams that I had watched as a kid in the '60s. He was the shortstop. I'd played with him in Triple A in Tulsa, when he was on the way out and I was on the way up. And then he was the third base coach here in St. Louis before he got the Houston job.

Having Hal down there made a lot of difference.

After I spoke to Dal and Whitey, I spoke to the Astros. They said I'd have a guaranteed contract for the next season, 1989.

So I decided to okay the trade.

I wasn't ready to quit. I wanted to see what another organization was like. Hal Lanier was the manager. My brother had played in Houston and he had liked it down there. And the Astros had a really good team that was going for a championship.

And they also had a great bunch of guys. Dave Smith. Mike Scott. Danny Darwin. Glenn Davis. Craig Reynolds. Alan Ashby. Juan Agosto was there too, before he came to the Cardinals.

And they had some radio announcer... Larry Dierker.

BAT BETRAYAL

People remember Larry Dierker because he later went from being a broadcaster to managing the Astros.

But he pitched here in St. Louis in '77. He broke his leg in spring training, but he pitched for us toward the end of the year.

My brother Kenny and Larry had played in Houston together. In '76, the year before Larry came over to us, Houston was in here for a series.

The first day in, Kenny asked if he could have one of my bats. So I gave him one—R-161 was the model number, and it was 36 inches, 34 ounces.

That's a big bat... but I was a big boy!

The second game of the series, I was pitching against Dierker. And he came up and hit a home run off me over the left field wall.

I never thought anything of it. I was just mad that I gave up a home run to the other pitcher.

Then in '77, Dierker came over. We were in spring training the first day, and he couldn't wait to run up to me and tell me that Kenny let him borrow my bat. And to tell me that was what he used to hit that home run off me.

Dierker said he was supposed to be sworn to secrecy and not to tell me. But he still couldn't wait to tell me all about it.

What can you do? I just figured my brother would use the bat for batting practice and stuff like that. He had his own bats, but you always try out other people's bats, too.

The next time I saw Kenny, I asked him about the whole deal. And his answer was:

"Dierker liked the bat. And he swore he'd never tell."

The guy hits a home run off me with my own bat, which my own brother gave to him.

And that was my brother's whole defense: The guy liked it and promised I'd never find out!

PLAYING HARDBALL

Steve Kline is also the Cardinals' player rep. It's a bad job, but somebody's got to do it.

Just check his stats when the Players' Association was doing the new bargaining agreement with the owners. It definitely affects your play. I know. I was one of our player reps in '81, when we had the strike and the split season. It just wears on you.

You're talking to the Players' Association in New York, and talking to your team and trying to explain the situation, and talking to the press and trying to explain it in a way that doesn't sound greedy.

In every walk of life, when people are negotiating they look greedy... on both sides of the table. Both sides want something that the other side has. That's what negotiations are all about.

In '74, before we had free agency, I got called up from the minors and was a regular starter for the last month of the season. My record was seven and four and my earned run average was just under three runs a game. That last month, my record was four and zero with no decisions in my other two starts. I was making the minimum big-league salary, which was $16,000.

That winter when the contracts came out, the Cardinals offered me a $2,000 raise to $18,000.

But the minimum went from $16,000 to $18,000. So it wasn't really a raise. It's what they had to offer me under the basic agreement between the players and the owners.

The contract wasn't even from Bing Devine, the general manager. I dealt with Jim Toomey, the public relations guy who also did the contracts for the younger guys.

I didn't care who I dealt with. I just wanted a contract.

We didn't have agents then, either. So I called my brother because he'd been in the big leagues for a couple seasons by then.

Kenny knew the ropes of shrewdly negotiating a contract... I thought!

Hey, when in doubt, look to your big brother.

Kenny told me to put the contract in an envelope and send it back. Unsigned. With no note. And don't call them.

I did what he said, but I worried at the same time. I mean, I'd only been there half a year, since July.

And Kenny said, "Don't worry. They'll call you."

This was December. About three weeks went by, and we were into January, and spring training is in February, and I heard nothing from the ball club. Nothing.

I was getting a little nervous. And finally, Jim Toomey sent me a contract for about $21,000. No explanation. Just a contract.

Oh, man! That thing was signed and on the way back before the ink dried on my signature.

But before free agency, that's just the way it worked.

CHECKING OUT AT SEASON'S END

In my rookie season, '74, the last series we played was in Montreal. And going into that series we were tied for first place in the division with Pittsburgh.

I was pitching the first game of the series—that's when Bob Gibson asked me if I was nervous—and I won.

The way it spun out, Gibson pitched the next game and lost. Mike Jorgensen, who later played for the Cardinals and was our farm director, hit a home run for Montreal.

Meanwhile, Pittsburgh won and was one game ahead of us. The next day in Montreal, we got snowed out of our last game of the year.

Instead of flying home immediately, we had to stay in Montreal in case the Pirates lost their last game at home against Chicago.

If the Pirates lost, we'd have to play a makeup game with the Expos the following day. If we won that makeup game, we'd have had a playoff game with Pittsburgh to see who went to the play-offs.

But the Cardinals didn't want to pay for our hotel an extra day in Montreal, because we might not need that makeup game the next day.

So we had to check out of our rooms that afternoon and wait in the lobby with all our stuff until we found out what Pittsburgh did.

The Pirates game wasn't broadcast on TV or radio in Canada. There was no ESPN and no Internet. Things were just different then.

Somebody on our team got on the phone and called some-body else who was listening to the game somewhere—or some-thing like that. Our guy would get the play-by-play over the phone and then relay it to us in the lobby.

We heard that Chicago went ahead and Rick Reuschel was pitching for the Cubs. He was their best pitcher. We heard that Reuschel struck out Bob Robertson, but the ball got away from the catcher, Steve Swisher—this was before we got Swish.

Robertson ran down to first base on the missed third strike, and Swish threw the ball away.

So Robertson, who wasn't the fastest runner to say the least, was safe at first. And Pittsburgh went on to win the ballgame. We didn't need a makeup game.

And that was the end of our season, sitting in a hotel lobby in Montreal.

PITCHING DARTS

My roommate in '74 was Jimmy Dwyer. He had been my roommate all through the minor leagues.

So that last day of the season, when we got snowed out in Montreal, we were still in our room before we had to check out. We were bored.

So we went out and bought a dart board. We took it back to the room and took the pictures down off the wall and put it up.

We played darts for like six hours. Then we checked out and found out that Pittsburgh won its game and clinched the division.

We got on the plane and flew home. And the next day, I couldn't even straighten my elbow. It was so sore from throwing all those darts.

It was just a rookie mistake, and I learned a valuable lesson. Oh, man, I thought my elbow was broken! I couldn't straighten it out for about a week. If we had made the playoffs, I wouldn't have been able to pitch.

Well, I would have gone out and pitched... or tried to pitch. And who knows what would have happened?

Just think what everyone would have said if I'd been unavailable because I'd been throwing darts.

At the time, it seemed so unlucky when Bob Robertson got to first base on that strikeout. That helped Pittsburgh win its last game and clinch the division ahead of us.

But looking back, maybe luck was on my side.

FATHERLY ADVICE

That last month of my rookie season, when I was unbeaten, one of the no-decisions I got was against Pittsburgh.

My father, Herb, was in the hospital back in Sacramento, having a stomach operation.

I got knocked out early, the first or second inning, and it was one of those deals where we came back. I think we ended up winning like 14-to-13.

I always called my dad after I pitched. So I called him, and he sounded like he was still on pain medication. I wanted to check on him to see how he was doing, but naturally he wanted to know how I did.

I said, "Dad, I pitched really bad but we won."

And he said, "What happened? Wasn't your curveball breaking?"

And I remember telling him, "Dad, the last one curved over the left field wall. Manny Sanguillen hit a hanging curveball for a home run."

And like all dads, he wanted to make me feel better. He said, "Well, you'll get him next time."

But what made me feel the best was knowing that my dad was okay.

Later on, I found out how to pitch to Manny Sanguillen.

I always figured, "Don't give him a good pitch to hit." But he was raking me down the left field line and he was raking me down the right field line.

So I asked my brother, "How do you get him out?"

Kenny said, "If you've got the nerve to do it, throw him a mediocre fastball, right down the middle of the plate."

I said, "Are you kidding?"

And Kenny said, "No. If you groove mediocre fastballs, he doesn't know whether to pull them or hit them to right field. And he'll pop them up."

I had nothing to lose. He was raking line drives off me already the way I was pitching him.

Now, a good time to try something new is when nobody's on base. That's when you always experiment. So the next time I pitched to Sanguillen with nobody on, I grooved a mediocre fastball.

And sure enough, he popped it up.

TRIAL BY ERROR

When I first came up, I threw the ball hard. I threw consistently over 90 miles per hour.

But when we played Cincinnati, people told me, "You can't throw the ball past Joe Morgan inside."

That was the scouting report.

Well, you have to test the water yourself. So you pick a situation—nobody on, two outs—where you can't get hurt. The first time Joe came up in that situation, I decided that I'd see whether the scouting report was right or not.

I thought I could get him between tics. He did that chicken wing thing with his elbow while he was waiting for the pitch in the batter's box.

Well, the scouting report was right. I threw a fastball inside, and Joe pulled it. Truthfully, Joe got around on it so fast that he pulled it foul.

You learn from your mistakes. I was just lucky it wasn't a bad mistake.

HAMMERIN' HANK

I got the chance to pitch against Hank Aaron in '74, when I was a rookie and he was still with Atlanta.

My first month in the big leagues, I pitched in the starting rotation. Then I went to the bullpen, even though I'd always been a starter in the minor leagues.

Red Schoendienst was our manager then and he called me into his office. Red gave me a choice. And what a stupid choice it was.

He said, "Go to the bullpen in the major leagues, or go back down to Triple A and start every fifth day."

Red had probably already made up his mind anyway, but it wasn't a rocket-science decision that I made. Of course I wanted to stay in the big leagues, no matter what I had to do.

So now I'm in the bullpen, and we're in Atlanta. Before the series, you go over the other hitters at a team meeting. And they tell us, "You can't throw a fastball past Hank Aaron, no matter how old he is."

He was about 40 years old then.

We start playing, and eventually I come in from the bullpen with the bases loaded and two outs. I'm 24 years old. I've been in the big leagues for a month.

And Hank Aaron's standing at home plate.

Ted Simmons is catching, and the first sign he puts down is a fastball on the outside part of the plate. I throw a perfect pitch, right into the glove.

Strike one, called.

So Teddy puts down the same thing. I throw a second perfect pitch, right into the glove.

Strike two, called.

The third pitch, Teddy called for a curveball, and it's a ball. So now I'm coming back with my fastball. I throw it, and it looks like the same thing as the first two fastballs... low on the outside corner.

This is my third perfect pitch to Hank Aaron!

And he hits the ball to straightaway center field. Bake McBride is out there playing deep, and he runs back to the fence. It's a chain-link fence about chest high, and Bake catches the ball right before it goes over the fence.

I felt good about getting Hank out. But it was hard to slap high-fives in the dugout when your center fielder just robbed him of a grand slam homer.

GQ JOE

The best prank I ever saw was probably when Tom Brunansky got Joe Magrane.

Joe was still real young, in his second or third year. He was a good-looking guy and he liked nice clothes. So Brunansky had someone send a telegram out of New York, pretending to ask Joe to do a photo shoot for *GQ* magazine.

The telegram said they'd have somebody get ahold of Joe in St. Louis. Then Brunansky got a photographer here in town to call Joe and set up a photo shoot.

The guy said he needed five different outfits for five different poses, and that they'd have the shoot before a game outside on the field at Busch Stadium. It was the middle of summer, which is really hot in St. Louis.

There were about 10 guys who knew what was going on that day. Joe had five suits hanging in his locker, but nobody said a word.

He and the photographer went out to start shooting, and we'd sneak out to look. Every time they changed to a different pose, Joe would come in and change to a different suit and tie. And he was sweating like a pig.

Joe Magrane... time for another GQ ensemble change?

Joe would be on the pitching mound, and the guy would take a bunch of shots. Then Joe would come in and change, and the guy would take him out to the left field fence sign for a few more shots.

At one point, he came in to change again and we said, "Joe, what's going on?"

He didn't want anybody to know what he was doing, so he just shrugged it off and said nothing.

A couple of weeks later, Joe was struggling a little bit.

We were in Atlanta, and Brunansky had another telegram sent to Joe from New York. It said something like, "Due to your recent substandard performances, we've chosen not to run the *GQ* photo spread with you."

Brunansky waited until there were a bunch of guys in the clubhouse to have the telegram delivered. So we were watching Joe open it.

And he read it without expression and just folded it up and put it in his pocket. And didn't say a word.

The next day, Brunansky has another telegram sent. It was something like:

Roses are red

Violets are blue

The joke's on you

There is no *GQ*.

Brunansky had that last telegram delivered to Joe with everyone in the clubhouse.

When Joe read it, he laughed and was angry at the same time for being duped. But he really took it well.

Actually, we were crushed that he didn't rant and rave. So he got back at us there!

But later, after I had left and was traded to Houston, Joe ended up having a real *GQ* photo spread.

I heard that he kept it a secret. Until one day, the guys came into the clubhouse, and there was a copy of Joe's *GQ* issue on everybody's locker chair.

So Joe did have the last laugh after all.

CLEVER KAAT

In baseball, there's a rule that you can't put a foreign substance on the ball.

Jim Kaat was the first pitcher I ever saw who doctored the ball. He used pine tar when he was here with the Cardinals.

At the beginning of the season, you have trouble with the ball because it's so cold. You use the rosin bag to get a better grip on the ball, but it doesn't work as well in the cold.

Jim Kaat... he could twist a rule like he could twist his elbow.

The best way to use rosin is to put it in your hands and rub them together real hard to heat it up. It kind of gets in the pores of your skin. But when it's cold, the pores don't open up.

Pine tar makes your fingers sticky, just as it does when a hitter puts it on the bat. It gives you a better grip, especially on a breaking ball.

Jim Kaat had pine tar that he put on his uniform, right on the front of his pants. You could see a dirty spot there. But he also chewed tobacco, so you couldn't tell what the stains were from.

Jim never got caught. But he had his defense all ready. His philosophy was:

"Read the label on the substance and make sure everything was made in the United States. That way, it isn't a foreign substance on the ball!"

THE DOCTOR IS IN

The first time I ever tried to throw a doctored ball was on the side, just practicing. It was about '84, probably.

I learned to throw it using K-Y Jelly. It wasn't real greasy and it was clear, so nobody could tell where you hid it on yourself.

The first time I ever tried to use it in a game was against the Cubs in Chicago. The first time you try it, you're sure that you'll get caught.

You swear everybody in the ballpark is watching you go to your special place to get it. And never mind where that was... I can't give away all my secrets!

And when I went to that special place the first time and put some K-Y on the ball, I knew I had too much. I knew I wouldn't be able to control it.

But it was the seventh inning or so and we were winning. I don't remember who the batter was, but I thought it would be a good time to try it.

*Here's Mike Roarke teaching me a
legal pitch... the splitter,* not *the spitter!*

And just as I moved my arm toward the plate, I knew I had
way too much stuff on the ball. Sure enough, I threw the pitch
up over the batter, the catcher and the umpire. The ball went all
the way to the backstop.

You know how they have that little brick wall behind home
plate at Wrigley Field? The ball caromed off that low wall and
bounced right back to the umpire. The ballboy didn't even have a
chance to get it.

The umpire—I don't remember who he was, either—just
started laughing. And he threw the ball out.

But I didn't throw it again that game. I knew I needed to
refine it a little bit.

TRUE CONFESSIONS

Late in my career, I did throw a doctored ball. Not very often. Just once in a while.

I just wanted another pitch, something that was offspeed and went down to the hitter, just as a split-fingered fastball would do. So I returned to K-Y Jelly.

And I got Mike Schmidt out with it once. He hit a fly ball to center field, and he was just shaking his head as he went back to the dugout.

He knew there was something wrong with that ball. Good hitters can pick up the rotation on the ball, and that ball that I threw Mike had a different rotation than he was used to seeing.

And when the hitters see rotation they haven't seen before, it makes them think that you have another pitch. The hitters don't know for sure how it got there, but it makes them think up there.

And the best thing was, it wasn't illegal. K-Y Jelly was made in the United States. I know, because I checked.

Jim Kaat had taught me to stay away from foreign substances. And that made it okay!

BAD BAT BOYS

People talk about pitchers cheating, but what about the hitters?

There was such a rash of illegal bats there for a while in the '80s, it seemed like every time somebody hit a ball off the end of the bat, the bat broke and Superballs would come bouncing out of the barrel.

Then there was Howard Johnson, when he was with the Mets. They were our big rivals and we were playing a series in St. Louis.

The thing was, Howard Johnson was a good player. He had a lot of ability. But he was in the league for four or five years and never hit more than 10 or 12 homers.

And then, all of a sudden, he was hitting more than 30.

So we got one of his bats somehow and X-rayed it in the medical room by the clubhouse. I don't know who did it—it wasn't me—but I'm sure Whitey had a hand in it.

They found that the bat was hollowed out. A lighter bat helps the hitter create quicker bat speed. And they marked it.

The next day, Howard got a home run or a big hit, and Whitey wanted the umpires to X-ray the bat. And the umpires wouldn't do it. They just gave the bat back to him.

We knew the X-rays would *not* be negative. Not on that bat! It had our mark on it. But we couldn't say how we knew. Because we weren't supposed to be sneaking a bat out of their clubhouse to check it.

I don't know why the umpires really didn't want to check balls and bats that they knew were doctored. It might be because a pitcher once threatened to sue the umpires if they accused him of cheating.

The umpires didn't think Major League Baseball was backing them, so they just looked away.

But umpires are a sort of funny breed, anyway. Obviously, they can influence the game. Period.

But after you've been in the game awhile, you realized that not only do you have to know the tendencies of the hitters, you also have to know the tendencies of the umpires.

AN UMPIRE'S GOOD DEEDS

I was pitching a game in Los Angeles, and Eric Gregg was behind home plate. It was his first or second year as an umpire.

The first two innings, I was throwing pitches that weren't inside or outside. They were right at the knees. And they were being called balls.

Doug Harvey, the crew chief, was at second base. In the top of the third inning, I reached second. And I said, "Doug, those pitches I threw... do you think they're low?"

He said, "They looked pretty good, but it takes an umpire a little time to settle into the strike zone."

And I said, "Doug, if he doesn't settle in soon, I won't be out here very long."

When the inning was over, Doug walked in and talked to Eric. I don't know what he said. All I know is that Eric suddenly settled in.

And those same pitches were suddenly strikes.

Another thing that Doug Harvey did for me was in my rookie season. I was starting to get in trouble in a game at home, giving up hits.

Apparently, I looked flustered. Doug was the second base umpire, and for no reason, he called time out and asked to see the baseball.

I flipped it to him. He just grabbed it and rubbed it up a little bit and walked over and put it in my glove. And he said, "Hey, you've got good stuff. Just settle down. You'll be all right."

I didn't know what to say. I just kept pitching, and I did settle down. I just needed a break from being flustered.

Doug Harvey gave me that break. And I never did find out why.

WHITEY AND THE LORD

Whitey and umpire Doug Harvey did not get along.

As I said before, I never had a problem with Doug. But Whitey always referred to him as "the Lord." He thought Doug was just a little pompous.

In '87, Joe Magrane was pitching in New York. He was a rookie then. The Mets were our big rivals, and we were in a pennant race with them.

It was lightly sprinkling when we were supposed to start. And the Mets obviously wanted to get the game in.

Once the lineup cards are handed to the umpires, they have the discretion to stop the game or not even start it. But they wanted to get the game in, so the umpires started the game in the rain.

The forecast was for more rain. And it kept raining. And they kept us playing.

The mound was just gooey and slippery. The ground crew would come out and put Diamond Dust, a drying agent, on it, but that stuff gets wet, too.

Joe was the future of the Cardinals, their future pitching star, and he could have gotten hurt in those conditions.

It kept raining, and the umpires wouldn't call the game.

After the fifth inning, a game is legal. We finished the fifth, and we were behind... and then Doug, the crew chief, called the game.

It wasn't raining any harder. I mean, it didn't seem any harder. When you're behind, the weather never seems as bad. You always need that one more at-bat.

And that really ticked Whitey off. And it didn't help his opinion of Doug Harvey.

Whitey with Paul Runge... thinking,
"Thank God it's not 'the Lord.'"

A STUPER MOVE

In the '82 World Series, we were down three games to two to the Brewers. We had to win the last two games.

John Stuper was a rookie, and he started Game 6, and he was winning. We were way ahead. Then we had a long rain delay, an hour and a half or two hours.

When we finally came back, I was surprised that Whitey brought him back to pitch. He asked Stupe, and Stupe said okay. He came back out and won, and that evened the series.

I'm sure Whitey did it because he wanted everybody available for Game 7. He didn't want to use a pitcher in a blowout if he could help it. You have all winter to rest.

After you're off for four or five months, your arm should be all right. But Stupe did have arm problems. And after two more years, he was gone.

I don't know for sure if the problems were because he came back after that long rain delay. And Whitey did ask him if he'd be okay.

But nobody's going to tell the manager that he can't pitch. Especially a young guy in a World Series game.

MY ANSWER MAN

Dave Ricketts was the coach who was here the longest when I was with the Cardinals. He had been a basketball star at Duquesne University and then had caught for the Cardinals.

He was an unbelievably good guy. And a great bullpen coach.

I went through so many pitching coaches in 15 years here: Barney Schultz, Bob Milliken, Claude Osteen, Hub Kittle, Mike Roarke. That's a new pitching coach every three years.

John Stuper... he won Game 6 of the '82
World Series with raindrops falling on his head.

David was the one person who saw me the most. And since he was the bullpen coach all that time, he really saw a lot.

Sometimes pitching coaches are a little too helpful. Finally, I got to where I'd tell them, "I can only work on one thing at a time."

You can't work on three things at once and expect to be able to release the ball—and still hit the catcher's glove.

When I'd get really in a funk, I'd go talk to Dave. We always did it when the pitching coach wasn't around.

We'd sit down on the bench in the bullpen, and Dave would always say the same thing:

"What is it that you think you need to do?"

So I'd talk through my whole motion. I'd show him where my hands should be at each part of the windup and the delivery.

And then he'd say, "Well, you're not doing that."

He'd pick out the one thing that was wrong with what I'd just got done explaining. Maybe my hands were too close to my body in the windup. Or I was throwing across my body on the delivery.

Then he'd flip me a ball and walk down to the plate in the bullpen. I'd get on the mound and throw, and he'd catch.

It was like the problem was solved—without me knowing that he was letting me solve the problem myself.

We probably did this at least once a year. And after the problem was solved, I'd always say, "Hey, David, thank you."

And he's always say, "Don't give me any of the credit... 'cause I'm not taking any of the blame!"

And we'd both laugh.

MR. RICKETTS

Dave Ricketts did the same thing with hitters that he did with me.

When George Hendrick's swing was messed up, he'd always go to David. And David would say:

"George, what are you trying to do?"

George would go through his swing and explain it to him. Then David would make a suggestion. And George would get in the cage while David threw batting practice to him.

It might only take 10 swings till George had his swing squared away, just like it might only take me 10 minutes of throwing on the side to get straightened out.

That's how good Dave Ricketts was.

He had the respect of a lot of players, especially the young players. They always called him Mr. Ricketts. Most of the guys kept calling him that even when they became veterans. I know George always called him Mr. Ricketts.

He was always David to me, and always had such a good rapport with the guys. Then again, he was a schoolteacher at one time.

He just had that calmness about him.

CHARGE ACCOUNTS

Bill Buckner was the only hitter who ever started out to the mound on me.

He was with the Cubs then and the game was at Wrigley Field. He was a left-handed hitter, so I turned the ball over to get it moving to the outside of the plate. And I threw him a lot of curves.

*I don't remember what happened
here... but I know it wasn't my fault!*

Buckner was creeping closer to the plate to be able to reach that outside pitch and that breaking ball. So then I threw him a fastball inside to get him off the plate. And it hit him.

He dropped his bat and started walking toward first base. All of a sudden he started over toward the mound. I threw my glove down and he just stopped and kept walking toward first base.

I don't know what made him stop, but that was the closest I ever got to somebody charging the mound.

BASEBRAWL

Nobody really fights during baseball fights. Well, hardly ever. And I don't know why.

When the benches clear, you just run out there with everyone and make sure nobody sucker-punches anybody.

Nobody really wants to start a brawl. Like Jay Johnstone, when he was with San Diego in '79.

He used to flip his bat at the ball and foul it off. He would actually let go of the bat to spoil a pitch he didn't like.

I got tired of seeing him do it all the time. I was pitching against him here in St. Louis. And he threw the bat at the ball and he fouled it off.

But when he let go of the bat, it helicoptered out to the mound. It hit and was sort of rolling toward me. So I picked it up and slammed it down on the artificial turf. And I broke it.

Johnstone just looked at it and went back and got another bat. So then he was ticked off.

Gene Tenace was playing for San Diego then. When Gene came over to the Cardinals a few years later, he told me that Johnstone between innings went up the runway from the dugout, took a bat and practiced throwing it for the next time he came up against me.

Just so he could throw it right back at me again.

Gene said that while Johnstone was practicing his bat throws in the runway, he almost hit one of his own pitchers, Randy Jones.

Randy was walking around the corner from the clubhouse and the bat just missed him.

So the next time Jay Johnstone came up against me, I threw him a pitch and he threw the bat again.

The umpire wasn't at all amused. I didn't break his bat this time because it didn't come anywhere close to me. So I wasn't that upset.

Johnstone got to throw it in my direction again. And that satisfied him—without having to charge the mound.

Jay Johnstone, explaining to John McSherry how his bat helicoptered at me twice in one game... as I said, it didn't bother me at all!

THE TECHNIQUE OF BREAKING A BAT

A couple of games after the Jay Johnstone bat-throwing contest, Pete Vuckovich was pitching for us. Another hitter threw his bat at the ball, and the bat ended up on the mound.

Vuke was a big guy, and he was going to do the same thing I did with Johnstone's bat: slam it down on the turf and break it.

But Vuke slammed it down and nothing happened. It just bounced off the turf. He ended up just flipping the bat back to the hitter.

Where Vuke messed up was, he should have slammed the bat with the label up. With the label up, it's easy to break, especially on Astroturf.

He tried to break it with the label on the side, where the grain is the strongest. That's the way hitters hold the bat when they swing so they don't break it.

When the inning was over, Vuke came back to the dugout and said, "I thought I'd be cool and break that bat, but it just wouldn't break."

I told him, "You have to have the label up."

And he said, "Oh... I didn't know there was a technique to it."

He didn't break that bat. But he did get good spring out of it when it bounced off the turf.

BROCK-A-BRAWLIN'

Even though he was a nice guy, Lou Brock was always in the middle of mean stuff. Like when he always slid hard into second base when he was stealing.

We were playing Montreal, and I think Tim Foli was playing shortstop. We played a Saturday game, and Lou slid hard into second base.

He always slid so late into a base—I guess so he could see where the ball was and kick it out of the glove if he had to.

So he and Foli had words. And all of a sudden, they were rolling around at second base. Lou had this quick left jab, and he was working it on Foli.

And then the dugouts and bullpens emptied.

That's back when we had Reggie Smith, and oh my gosh, what a build he had. Reggie was just pulling people off the pile, and then all of a sudden Reggie got his face scratched.

Nobody knew for sure who did it. Reggie thought it was Dave Bristol, who was coaching for the Expos. So then Reggie and Bristol started going at it.

That finally got broken up. But as Reggie and Bristol got pulled apart, Reggie yelled, "You fight like a woman!"

That's a baseball brawl.

After that Saturday fight against Montreal, we still had to play a Sunday day game. This was '74 or '75, because Red Schoendienst was still managing us.

Before the game that Sunday, Dave Bristol took the lineup card out to the umpires at home plate. Reggie Smith saw Bristol going out, so he asked Red if he could take the lineup card out for us.

Red didn't think anything of it, or maybe he just wasn't thinking. But I knew something would happen. So I went out to the dugout to watch.

It was just Reggie and Bristol and the four umpires. All of a sudden, right there at home plate, Reggie and Bristol got into another fight.

A lot of guys weren't even out of the clubhouse yet, so the benches didn't empty. The umpires broke it up by themselves.

The amazing thing is, Bristol got kicked out of the game—and Reggie didn't. I couldn't figure that out.

How can you get kicked out of a game before it even starts? I couldn't figure that out either.

That was the first time I'd ever seen that. And I never saw it again.

HIGH JUMP HIJINKS

One time, in Red's last year of managing, we were in Pittsburgh. Back then they didn't broadcast a lot of games on TV. But this was a Sunday day game being televised back home to St. Louis.

We were losing, and it was about the seventh inning or so. The game was pretty much not interesting, I guess, for the people back home. So the broadcasters had to fill in.

The bullpens at Three Rivers Stadium were angled back in the corners by the foul poles, where the seats would end. There was a pie-shaped wedge of seats that stuck out.

The manager couldn't see out into his own bullpen from the dugout, and the broadcasters couldn't see the bullpen from the booth, either.

The broadcasters were trying to fill in and make the game seem semi-exciting so that the viewers didn't tune out. One of the cameramen panned our bullpen and showed our relief pitchers.

They had set up a high-jump standard, and the camera caught all of that action. One of the relievers, Eddie Solomon, was trying to jump over the bar.

Jay Randolph was one of the broadcasters. When Eddie came on the monitor, Jay said, "Since this is an Olympic year, apparently they're practicing for the Olympics."

Bing Devine, our general manager, was watching on TV back in St. Louis. And Bing was not amused. He was angry with Red and said something to him. Red was angry and passed it on to us.

Apparently Eddie got the gold medal—and a ticket out of town. Because that was his only season with us.

CARNIVAL TIME

Mike Tyson—the infielder, not the boxer—and I were good friends when he played here.

Mike played shortstop for us and then he moved over to second base when Garry Templeton got here.

I'd been pitching for the Cardinals for three or four years, and Mike and I had kids the same age. One time when we had an off day, our families decided to go out to Six Flags amusement park together and enjoy the day.

You know that game where you throw the ball and break some plates to win a prize?

They had one of those games at Six Flags. Mike and I decided to win something for the kids. So we get the baseballs, and I hit one out of three plates.

There were two little kids standing behind me when I was throwing. And when I get done, I heard one kid say to the other kid:

"See? I *told* you that wasn't Bob Forsch!"

EAR'S HOW YOU DO IT

Mark Littell was a relief pitcher we got from Kansas City for Al Hrabosky. I pitched against Mark in the minor leagues, and he was just unhittable then.

Mark was deaf in one ear. I found out because my locker was on his bad side. I'd talk to him and get no response. Then one day, he finally told me he couldn't hear out of that ear.

One day, I saw him talking on the phone in the clubhouse. It was noisy in there. And he had the phone up to his good ear, and he had his finger in his bad ear.

I said, "Mark, what are you doing?"

He said, "What do you mean?"

I said, "You've got your finger in your bad ear to block out the noise."

And Mark said, "Well, I see everyone else doing it."

He was dead serious.

So that was good enough for me, I guess.

MAKING A SPLASH

Mark Littell was just a country boy from around Cape Girardeau, down near the Missouri Bootheel. We used to go fishing together.

One time, we went down over the All-Star break to trout fish at Lake Taneycomo, down by Table Rock Lake near the Ozarks. Our families went down with us.

We each rented a little boat with an outboard motor on it so we could take our families out with us. It was maybe a 10-horsepower motor, and the guy at the boat dock told us how to run it.

I was listening, because I'd never run one before. Mark said he had. Since I was unsure, I wanted to back my boat up first so they could talk me through it.

So I backed my boat up out of the slip and got out on the lake.

Then Mark put his boat in reverse. But he gunned the motor and rammed his boat into another boat in a different slip. And he almost knocked his wife out of their boat.

After that fiasco was over, he and I went out together the next day without the families. We decided to get a fishing guide and fish for crappie.

We were out on the lake, the three of us all in the guide's boat. And Mark was standing on the very tip of the boat. I wasn't paying attention—I was busy fishing—and all of a sudden I heard this big splash.

I looked on the water and there was Mark.

He still had his cap on. His fishing pole was still in his hand. And he was treading water with a big plug of chewing tobacco in his mouth.

I asked him what happened, and Mark just said, "I fell in."

After Mark fell in the water, we got him back in the boat. Our guide was just cracking up.

So we went back in to shore. Mark dried off and the guide was cleaning and filleting the fish. Mark was begging this guy to let him help clean them.

The guide finally said okay. So Mark started using the guide's knife to cut out the rib bone and flip it in the water.

Mark got down to the last of the fillets, and instead of throwing the rib bone into the water, he accidentally threw the guide's knife.

So in the same day, the poor guide had to fish Mark out of the water and then lost his fillet knife.

Mark did buy him a new knife. And I knew the guide was probably thinking, "I'm with two major-league baseball pitchers, and they're the worst fishermen in the world!"

But, hey, we did catch fish.

THE LINE ON LITTELL

Line drives scare pitchers. You always have that fear of getting hit on the mound.

Every once in a while, you wake up in the middle of the night, dreaming that you got hit by a baseball.

Mark Littell was a right-hander who had a really good slider. He was pitching in Los Angeles one time, and somebody hit a line drive back up the middle.

The ball just hit him right on the forehead and his cap went flying. It was like watching one of those westerns where the cowboy gets his hat knocked off by a bullet.

The ball bounced off his head and landed way out in center field, right in front of the outfielder. That's how hard that ball was hit, and how hard it Mark.

And the thing is, he didn't even go down. That's how tough Mark Littell was.

POPS

A pitcher can tell where the ball will be hit when the pitch is on the way to home plate.

You know that a good pull hitter will try to pull an outside pitch, so the ball will end up going right up the middle. Right through the mound.

I threw a pitch once to Willie Stargell. Once I saw that big bat start to go around, I knew where that ball was going.

Right at me.

I was a little sideways in my follow-through, and he hit a line drive right back at my side. I caught it just before it caught me in my ribs.

Willie didn't even have time to drop the bat. But he actually started out toward the mound to see if I was all right. His teammates on the Pirates called him Pops, and I can see why. Just like a father, he was going to make sure I was all right, even though I was on the other team.

He was just a classy man. Dave Ricketts told me that Willie's biggest fear was that he'd hurt a pitcher with a line drive.

Believe me, that was my biggest fear, too!

THE LUMBER COMPANY

The day I pitched, I always went out to watch the other team take batting practice. Especially on the road. I just wanted to see how they were swinging that day.

One time in the 1970s, I was getting ready to pitch in Three Rivers Stadium. The Pirates had Willie Stargell, Dave Parker, Bob Robertson, Bill Robinson, Al Oliver, guys like that. This was when aluminum bats first came out. These guys were taking batting practice, and I was hearing this new sound.

Ping! Ping! Ping!

They were using aluminum bats in BP. And they were laughing and counting their home runs.

But they didn't even count them if they barely went over the wall. In Three Rivers, there was this 20- or 30-foot space between the wall and the seats in the outfield. They were only counting the home runs that went into the seats. And measuring them against each other.

I was in awe of how these guys were hitting the ball. They were breaking seats. And then I thought to myself, "This is depressing. You've got to pitch against these guys."

So I just went back inside the clubhouse and had another cup of coffee.

The Pirates were called the Lumber Company back then. But that night, they were the Aluminum Company.

HEAVY METAL

Major League Baseball can never go to aluminum bats in the big leagues. It would be way too dangerous for a pitcher. There is no way a pitcher could get out of the way of those line drives. You're just 60 feet, six inches away from home plate.

I always laugh when they call third base the hot corner. A third baseman is 90 feet away from the plate. If he's up on the grass, he's more like 80 feet away.

A pitcher is 60 feet away—but that's at the start of your windup. By the time you let the ball go and you follow through, you're 50 feet away. And you're not set to field the ball, either.

I guess that's why the pitcher's rubber is called "the slab."

IN STITCHES

They switched from horsehide to cowhide baseballs in the '70s. And the first ones didn't have the tanning of the cowhide down well enough.

I was pitching on a rainy night once here at Busch Stadium, and I got a ball back that had been hit on the ground for an out. The ball was wet and the cover felt loose.

I was thinking, "Better for me! That ball won't go as far."

Dave Parker was up next, and he always hit the ball hard. I threw him a pitch, and he pounded that ball down into the ground on the artificial turf. It kept going up the middle for a hit.

And he ripped the cover off the ball. It looked like a tongue lapping the ground as it went by me.

When that ball came back to me, I just started laughing. Obviously, I wasn't throwing that ball again.

SEAMS TO MAKE SENSE

People always ask why I tugged at the ball with my fingernails when I was pitching.

I would lift up the seams of the ball. The seams are what give the ball movement. It's air resistance over the seams that can make the ball move.

The seams are raised off the cover, so you also use them to grip the ball better. It's better to use the seams than the flat surface.

If you get a new ball from the umpire that doesn't feel right, it's usually because the seams are just too flat. So I'd toss the ball back and ask for a new one.

I started tugging on the seams because I got tired of throwing the ball back to the umpire. I'd just lift the seams up with my fingernails. And there's nothing illegal about that. But for a while, the hitters would ask to have the ball checked. The umpires would ask for the ball and then throw it back to me. Eventually, they just gave up and quit doing that. They knew I wasn't doing anything wrong.

BIG HEART

This shows you how big Joaquin Andujar's heart is.

At the end of the every season that he was here in St. Louis, he asked all the guys for the equipment that they weren't taking home.

Shoes, gloves, sweatshirts, caps, anything. There was a lot of stuff. You always have three or four pairs of shoes that were semi-worn but not old. All the stuff was like that.

He'd throw it all in boxes and ship them back home to the Dominican Republic. Then he'd give them to all the needy kids down there. And they were all needy.

That showed us that he wasn't that "tough Dominican" that everyone thought he was. And that he wanted everyone to think he was.

WINTER BALL

I went to the Dominican Republic to play in the winter of '74.

The Cardinals wanted me to go. When you were young then, their whole premise was: you need to pitch. And you need to pitch against a better caliber of people.

They talk about kids watching their innings now. But what about this?

I was in Triple A at Tulsa and I threw 166 innings. We got done on September 1. Then I went down to winter ball and pitched for four months, from October till the playoffs ended in January. I probably got a hundred more innings there.

I had a couple weeks off and went to spring training in February. I pitched there, and then I went back to Tulsa in April and threw 103 innings till I got called up to St. Louis in July.

Then I threw another hundred innings in the big leagues till the end of the season.

Not counting what I threw in spring training, that's 470 innings from April to September of '74. That's a year and a half. And I was 23, 24 years old.

And the thing about it is that after that season, the Cardinals actually asked if I wanted to go back to winter ball. How stupid was that?

My feeling was: "And do what?"

First of all, I was too tired of putting the uniform on. And second of all, my arm would never, *never* have held up.

Today, they wouldn't even consider that. I mean, how many guys go to winter ball? You don't read about too many rookies who do that.

Maybe their thinking had something to do with building arm strength. Either that or the strong survive... and the weak just don't make it.

VISA PROBLEMS

I played for a team in Santo Domingo, which is the capital of the Dominican Republic. But I had never been to winter ball before. I didn't know how it worked.

Before we went down, we were told that all we had to do was get a 15-day work visa, that we didn't need a passport—and that once we got there we would turn over our visa to the owner of our team and that he would renew it.

The reality was, we found out once we got there that you couldn't go home until the season was over. The owner wouldn't give your visa back until then.

They'd had a problem with Americans leaving early. A player might not like the conditions, go home for Thanksgiving or Christmas and never return.

So when the owner kept your visa, that eliminated his problem. There was no getting out early.

CAST OF CHARACTERS

Al Hrabosky was on our team in Santo Domingo. So were Gary Mathews and Garry Maddox, who were outfielders for the Giants. And Jim Dwyer, my roommate from all through the minor leagues. And Craig Skok, who was with Boston just a short time.

We also had Matty Alou and Juan Marichal, who were Dominicans. They played about one or two games a season. That's it. If you were a native, it was like you belonged to an organization over there. You had to stay with the one club. Or they could trade you to another club—just like the big leagues do with American players.

Our manager got fired and they hired Felipe Alou. That could have been his first managing job in baseball.

I liked Felipe. He was a player's manager. He treated all of us like big-leaguers.

And I think his son, Moises, might have been one of the little kids shagging balls for us in the outfield.

There were three other teams in the Dominican winter league when I was there. One of them was in Santo Domingo, too, and it was more or less part of the Los Angeles Dodgers organization.

Our team wore red and their team wore blue. They looked just like the Dodger uniforms, except they didn't say Dodgers on them.

Steve Garvey played first base for them. Steve Yeager caught. Teddy Martinez played second and Vaughn Joshua played right. I think Ron Cey might have been there, too.

They had the whole future Dodger team, with Tommy Lasorda managing them.

This was when Tommy was still a minor-league manager. He spoke Spanish fluently, and he was big down there. Oh my gosh, he was an idol down there!

A WINTER ALL-STAR

On New Year's Day down there in the Dominican, we played an All-Star Game between the best Americans and the best Dominicans from the four teams.

I was picked to play. The night before was New Year's Eve, and naturally we were having a party. Forgetting about the All-Star Game, I had way too much to drink.

The next day when we got to the ballpark, I was sick to my stomach. I felt terrible.

Tommy Lasorda was managing the American All-Star team. So I said, "Tommy, I can't pitch. I think I've got the flu."

He said, "I only need two innings." I was in no shape to pitch, but he shamed me into going out there.

Tommy Lasorda said he wanted to pitch Al Hrabosky two innings, me two innings and Craig Skok two innings.

We were the three best starters on our team in Santo Domingo, and we were pitching the first six innings. Tommy said he would use his pitchers to fill out the rest of the game. Which was only three innings.

Now, it's important to point out that our Dominican team was opening a series the next day with Tommy's team. It was a huge rivalry.

So the All-Star Game started. Hrabosky pitched his two innings. Then it was my turn. I went out to take my warmup pitches, walked behind the mound and threw up. That's the kind of shape I was in.

I don't know if Tommy saw that, but it didn't matter. I was pitching—he was clear about that. So I pitched my two innings, and I didn't give up any runs.

Skok came in and pitched his two innings. But then Tommy didn't pitch any of his regular guys. He had one pitcher on his reserve list, and he put him in.

So our three top starters had just warmed up and pitched two innings each. Tommy had his best pitchers all rested. And our two teams were going for first place the next day.

It took us three days to get our pitching rotation squared away. So his team won the series. Anything to win. And he did win the winter league title that year.

Two years later, Tommy Lasorda was managing the Dodgers.

NO PLACE LIKE HOME

You could say that things were different in the Dominican Republic.

They never, ever had any hot water in any of the shower rooms in the clubhouse. I wouldn't even try to shower there. I'd just take my uniform off, get dressed in my street clothes and go back to our hotel to shower.

The clubhouse floors were slat boards. They didn't fit flush against each other. There were spaces between the boards.

We were told not to eat the food for sale outside the stadium for fear of the cooking—or lack thereof. They would sell lobsters and stuff outside the stadium, but the native players didn't have a problem with the food.

They would buy the lobsters and bring them into the clubhouse and eat them. They'd throw the lobster shells on the floor, the way we throw peanut shells on the floor of a bar up here.

But these ants would come up through the floorboards to get at the lobster shells. All of a sudden, they'd be all over your legs. It'd be like a feeding frenzy on your legs, not the shells. Those ants would bite. And, oh yeah, it hurt!

But you got angry more than anything at the sanitary conditions. Or lack thereof.

And it seemed like it never bothered the native players. Probably because they were throwing the lobster shells over near the stupid American players!

LIGHTS OUT

The Dominican Republic was such a poor country. When we were there, the city of Santo Domingo did not have enough electrical power.

For batting practice before night games, they would only light the standards behind home plate. So the only lighting was in the infield.

You'd be out shagging flies, and you could see the ball being hit. After it left the bat, you knew if it'd be coming at you... but you had no idea exactly where it was.

The incredible thing about it was, the Dominican players who shagged flies would never miss one. They could see the ball at night with no lights. That's how good they were.

Meanwhile, I couldn't get off the field fast enough after batting practice for fear of being hit.

Then when the game would start, they'd have to black out an area of town. They'd just shut off the power in a certain area so they could turn on all the stadium lights for three hours.

The people in town didn't seem to resent it. Most of them didn't have electricity anyway. The others didn't care. They just expected that the lights would go out for a while on some nights.

Baseball in the Dominican was life. That's how people got out of there and out of their poverty.

THE BOTTOM LINE

When I look back, that year of winter ball was really good for me.

I got to face some good competition. Tommy Lasorda had all those future Dodgers on his team. Bill Madlock was down there on another team. So was Dave Parker.

Even though I started the next year in Triple A at Tulsa, winter ball really did prepare me. When the Cardinals called me up in July of that season, I was ready.

I never returned to the minors again. Or to the Dominican, even though the Cardinals wanted me to go back the next winter.

YOU BET

One thing about the Dominican fans when I was there: they bet on everything at the ballpark.

When an inning was over, they'd bet on whether the ball ended up on the dirt or the grass when somebody rolled it to the mound.

I didn't even realize it when I played for the Cardinals, but some people down at Busch Stadium do the same thing.

When I retired and first started going down to watch games there, I was shocked. After each inning, when somebody rolled the ball toward the mound, some fans actually bet on whether the ball ended up on the mound or stayed on the grass.

I guess I was naive.

And I guess I could have made a lot of money rolling the ball onto the dirt when I was out there!

But every season, someone from Major League Baseball or the Cardinal office would come into the clubhouse and read a statement from the commissioner about not betting on games.

And it was posted in every clubhouse, home and on the road.

So no players can say they didn't know about not betting on baseball or any other sport.

You have to be careful. Everyone knows that.

When I played, I had people calling my hotel room on the road to find out how I felt. These were total strangers. They'd never give their names, but they were obviously gamblers.

They'd always ask, "How do you feel?"

I always wanted to say, "With my hands!"

My standard answer was, "Fine. How are you feeling?" And then I'd hang up.

The thing is, if you're approached by someone suspicious, you're supposed to call your league office.

But how can you report that? This was before caller ID.

There was nothing to report.

ME VS. CHARLIE HUSTLE

I actually did pretty well pitching against Pete Rose.

He was approaching Stan Musial's record for career hits in the National League. He was with the Phillies then and we were flying to Philadelphia for the first game after the strike ended.

He needed one hit to get Stan's record. I was scheduled to pitch the first game of the series.

On the flight to Philly, a sports writer from St. Louis came to the back of the plane. He told me that he already had his story written that I would be the one to give up the record hit to Pete Rose.

I said, "No, I won't."

Quite honestly, he was not going to get that hit off me.

Between giving him a good pitch to hit or walking him, I would walk him every time—unless it was a critical situation.

And he didn't get a hit off me. I think he went zero for three. I didn't want to be a baseball trivia question.

THE BULLPEN

Warming up in the bullpen is an art. That's why it's so tough for a starter to go to the bullpen and become a reliever.

A starter's used to throwing 15 minutes before the game. And he knows when he's going to pitch.

When you're a reliever, you're rushed to get loose as quick as you can in the bullpen. And then your team may get out of the inning and you aren't used, so you go sit down again.

You don't know when you'll be getting up again, unless you know the manager and how he uses pitchers.

Whitey Herzog was great at handling a pitching staff.

When Whitey filled out the lineup card and hung it on the dugout wall before the game, he listed the pitchers and the pinch hitters in the order that they'd be used.

If you were a pitcher on the top of the list—which meant you would be in for long relief—your responsibility was innings one through five. That's when you might be used.

After that, you had the middlemen—the setup men—and then you had your closer. So there was no confusion about what your job was when you went down to the bullpen.

If your designated innings were over and you weren't used, you could kick back and enjoy the rest of the game. It was somebody else's job coming up.

NO BULL IN THE PEN

In the bullpen, you don't have time to warm up and watch the game at the same time.

That's why you need a good bullpen coach. He'll tell you situations that are happening in the game. He'll also have a feel for what the manager will do.

Once you're loose, he knows whether there's any need for you to keep throwing or not.

Even if you're still within your framework of innings when the manager might need you, if you're loose, you're loose. You won't get any looser.

All you'll do is wear your arm out before you get in the game. Or wear it out for the next game if you don't pitch that time.

That's why you need a good bullpen coach, which David Ricketts was.

David knew every reliever well enough to know if you were ready to go in the game. And he knew when the manager wanted every reliever.

If a righty and a lefty were warming up, David would know who the on-deck hitter was. And he'd know if the hitter was a righty or lefty, because a right-handed pitcher will come in to face a righty, and a lefty will come in to face a lefty.

David knew that every pitcher's instinct is to go overboard to be loose when called upon. So when David thought you were loose, he'd just take the ball away. He'd do that all the time to Jeff Lahti.

David was always watching out for you. He had your interest at heart. And that's a great bullpen coach.

MINOR NO-NOS

My premise going into a baseball game was always the same: don't give up a run.

I never went into a game thinking about throwing a no-hitter. Never. At any level.

I threw two in the minor leagues. The first was a seven-inning game with Arkansas when I was in Double A. It was against Memphis, which was in the Mets organization.

In the minors back then, when you played a doubleheader you only played seven-inning games.

Then at Tulsa in Triple A, I pitched a nine-inning no-hitter against Denver, which was Houston's farm team.

I don't have the baseballs from my two minor-league no-hitters. They don't have baseballs to waste.

BIG-LEAGUE NO-NO

People think it's strange that I don't remember all the details about my no-hitters.

I can remember a bad pitch that somebody hit a home run on more than all the stuff that happened in my no-hitters.

Truly, I can remember bad things better than good things.

I guess it's called learning by your mistakes.

The first no-hitter that I pitched in the big leagues was in 1978.

But the game before that was probably one of the best I ever pitched. It was against Pittsburgh in St. Louis. It was one of those games where you feel good, you feel overpowering. And for me, that's a stretch.

My parents were here for the Pittsburgh game, and I really felt proud. By far, that was the best game they had ever seen me pitch. I went the distance and I think it was a three-hitter.

And then my folks went back home to Sacramento.

My next start was on April 16 and it was cold. We were playing Philadelphia at Busch Stadium and only about 11,000 fans were there.

I'm not sure whether it was the weather or the starting pitcher who caused such a small crowd.

I really didn't feel good warming up in the bullpen before the game. My arm just felt weak, like I'd spent it all the game before.

But it was amazing. The Phillies just kept hitting ball after ball... right at someone. Not particularly hard, but right at someone. I think I only had three strikeouts.

You don't even think about a no-hitter until after the sixth inning, when you only have to go through the lineup one more time. I was in a good situation because I had something like a three-run lead, which gives you wiggle room.

And I needed it in that game.

During that no-hitter, there was a questionable scoring decision on a ball hit down to Kenny Reitz at third base. I think it was the seventh inning.

I knew I had a no-hitter. So did everybody who was there. Naturally, everybody in the stadium was watching the scoreboard to see whether it was called a hit or an error.

Immediately, Neal Russo of the *St. Louis Post-Dispatch*—who was the official scorer—called it an error.

I later asked Neal about it. Neal was a really smart man. He used to make up crossword puzzles—not do them, make them up—while he was watching games in the press box.

And Neal probably had the best explanation I've ever heard from an official scorer. He told me, "That far along in the game, the first hit has to be a clean hit."

So I had my first big-league no-hitter.

Since then, it's amazing how many people have come up to me and said they were at that game.

I know I've signed more than 11,000 tickets!

*The scoreboard says 11,435 fans saw my first
no-hitter... and I say I've signed every one of their tickets!*

A HALL OF FAME NO-NO

I've got the baseballs from my two major-league no-hitters—
even though you're supposed to give the baseball and your cap to
the Hall of Fame.

I gave them a game ball each time. All the balls that they
throw out of the game are game balls, right?

But I kept the balls from the last outs.

You think the Hall of Fame will be coming after me now?

LEFT-RIGHT COMBINATION

The best lefty-righty duo we had in the bullpen, by far, was Ken Dayley and Todd Worrell.

Worrell, the right-hander, was the more overpowering. He was six foot five and he made it look easy.

Dayley, the left-hander, threw hard for someone five foot 10. And he had a better curveball than Worrell.

Most of the time, it didn't really matter if they faced a right-handed hitter or a left-handed hitter. They could get either one out.

But there was a situation once where Worrell was in the game with a left-hander coming up, and Whitey brought Dayley in. Instead of taking Worrell out, Whitey put him in right field.

After Dayley finished pitching to the left-handed hitter, a righty was coming up. So Whitey took Dayley out of the game and brought Worrell back in from right field.

I remember watching this and thinking, "Whitey, either you think a lot of those two guys... or you don't have a very good right fielder if you can replace him with a pitcher!"

A welcome sight in the bullpen... Dave Ricketts,
Mike Roarke and Todd Worrell (left to right).

STRAWBERRY'S ALARM CLOCK

Coming down to the wire in '85, we were playing the Mets in a big series at home. Kenny Dayley was pitching to Darryl Strawberry in a key situation.

And Strawberry hit a line drive off the clock in right center field. Game over. Loss.

Reporters can come up with some stupid questions after a game. And after this one, a reporter actually asked Kenny, "When did you know it was a home run?"

And Kenny just looked at him and said, "When it hit the clock."

Later, it was Kenny who got the save against the Dodgers in the playoffs when Jack Clark hit the game-winning home run off Tom Niedenfuer.

RUNNING WITH BARNEY SCHULTZ

Barney Schultz was my first major-league pitching coach when I came up to the Cardinals in 1974.

Growing up in Sacramento, I saw him pitch in the '64 World Series for the Cardinals against the Yankees.

Obviously, that makes an impression on you, having a pitching coach that you watched as a kid. It did for a while, anyway.

Pitching coaches always want you to run between starts. But Barney Schultz had this thing about having pitchers run after baseballs for conditioning.

You'd start at one foul line, usually in right field, and you'd all have your glove and a baseball. You'd run past Barney and flip him the ball and you'd keep running across the outfield, toward the other foul line.

He'd throw the ball up there in front of you. You were supposed to catch it before it hit the ground. And he'd lead you far enough that you had to sprint to catch the ball, much like a quarterback would lead a receiver with a pass.

I had two problems with that drill.

One, I am not built for speed. Two, I am real stubborn.

Actually, I had three problems: Barney Schultz was my equal in stubbornness.

Barney would get the pitchers together to run, and when it was my turn he'd lead me with a throw. But I wouldn't sprint. I'd just keep jogging.

The ball would go way over my head and start rolling. If we were home at Busch Stadium, the ball would roll on that plastic grass all the way over to the other corner.

I would just keep my same gait and go all the way over and pick up my baseball. It took me so long that the other pitchers would be lined up now on the left field foul line, ready to do it again the other way.

By the time I got back to the line, keeping my same gait, it was my time to go back the other way.

And Barney Schultz would lead me too far again, and the ball would go way over my head and roll to the other corner, and I'd keep my same gait and go pick it up.

Every night, we'd do 20 of these tests of who's the most stubborn.

He'd always say, "All you have to do is speed up."

And I'd always say, "All you have to do is throw it shorter."

Actually, I did get in good shape. When I started a game, I was ready to go the distance.

Because when I ran with Barney Schultz, I was building stamina, not speed.

THANKS FOR THE TIP

Before a game, you go over the opposing hitters with the pitching coach. We were playing the Astros my first season at Busch Stadium, and Barney Schultz said, "Art Howe is a fastball hitter. In a crucial situation, try to get him out with a breaking ball."

So I'm pitching late in the game. The Astros have the winning run on second base. And Art Howe comes up.

I'm thinking, "Crucial situation. Gotta get him out with a breaking ball."

So I throw him a hanging curveball. He hits it between third and shortstop for a base hit. And the winning run scores.

We fly to Pittsburgh after the game, and the next morning I'm in the hotel dining room having breakfast. The place is full. I'm sitting at a table by myself, with an empty seat, and Barney Schultz comes in.

Barney says, "Can I sit down?"

I say sure. Because I'm a nice guy... and I'm 24 years old and he's the pitching coach!

After some small talk, he says, "How can you throw Art Howe a curveball?"

I say, "Barney, when we went over everybody in the meeting, you said, 'In crucial situations, get him out with a curveball.'"

And Barney says, "What's your best pitch?"

I answer, "Fastball."

And he says, "Then how can you throw him a curveball?"

I say, "Because you told me to."

And he says, "If you had it do over again, what would you throw him?"

I say, "A curveball. But I wouldn't hang it."

And he says, "You're so stubborn. You'll never make it as a pitcher."

I wound up pitching 16 years in the big leagues. So I guess Barney was wrong about that last part.

And I never saw the logic in the other part.

If you're supposed to throw your best pitch in every crucial situation, why have all those meetings to go over the hitters?

And if you always rely on your best pitch, won't everybody walk up to home plate looking for your best pitch in a crucial situation?

I never did understand that.

LOGIC 102

Barney also had a thing about always keeping your elbow covered on your throwing arm. And that's what you should do when it's cool outside.

But in July in St. Louis, when you're running in the out-field—even the way I ran—it's too hot to keep a sweatshirt on. I didn't even wear a T-shirt underneath my jersey when it was hot. You sweat so much and the T-shirt gets too heavy.

Jim Kaat had the best philosophy on that. He said, "Hey, you come to the ballpark with a short-sleeve shirt on. You leave the ballpark with the same short-sleeve shirt on. Why do you need a long-sleeve shirt only when you have a uniform on?"

Especially when you look over and see Bob Gibson pitching in a short-sleeve shirt. It didn't seem to hurt his career.

GIBSON'S LISTS

Barney Schultz never made Bob Gibson run—ever—because his knees were so bad.

And I don't ever remember Gibby throwing on the side between starts. But he took ground balls at shortstop. Every day.

You didn't have to worry about Gibby being ready. He just prepared so well.

On his day of pitching, he didn't want to talk to anyone. He was mean when he came into the clubhouse. He had no friends that day, not even on his own team.

When you think about the incredible 1.12 earned run average he had in 1968, that will never be duplicated.

Neither will his complete games. In '68, he started 34 games and completed 28. The next year, he started 35 and completed 28. You won't see that again, either.

Not in today's era of shorter fences and livelier baseballs.

Bob Gibson was a hard man. I knew that he was a great competitor before I got to the Cardinals. But when I got called up, I found out he was *really* hard.

There was a chalkboard on the wall in the clubhouse in St. Louis. The coaches used to write down what time you're to be dressed for the game, announcements, things like that.

In '74, on the last homestand of my rookie year, Gibby went over and made two lists on the chalkboard.

The first consisted of guys who had a chance to come back the next year. The other list was the guys who were gone.

It was just his opinion. Apparently he had done it every year.

And the incredible thing is, the following year he was usually pretty right on target. I know he was right on the one year he did it when I was there.

All I know is, he had me coming back in '75. So I thought the list was great!

THE FAMILY CLAUSE

Not so much now, but years ago if you held out for a no-trade clause, people thought you were a baby.

The thinking was: "You're making a lot of money to play a game... and you still want a no-trade?"

But it's important if you have a family.

If you live in one place for a while and you really enjoy it, and your kids are in school, and you're all settled in, you can still walk into the clubhouse and find out that you've been traded. And you have to be there in three days.

So you go and your family stays behind, maybe for the rest of the season.

Even if you stay with one team almost all your career, like I did, you can't be there for a lot of stuff your kids do.

You're on the road for half the season. And when the team is home, you're still missing birthdays and school plays and all the stuff that happens in the evening, because you play at night so much.

But at least you're still there to support your kids before and after their activities.

My kids went to a private school in St. Louis and they didn't have school buses to ride. So when the team was home, I drove them to school every morning.

That was really the only time I got to see them except for weekends and summer vacation.

I'd leave for the ballpark before they got home from school, and they'd be asleep by the time I got home.

My daughters, Amy and Kristin, had trouble dealing with trades even before I finally got sent to Houston after almost 15 years here.

*Kristin (left) and Amy... just hanging
around spring training with their dad.*

Photo courtesy of Bob Forsch

They would be making friends with the kids of other players through the course of the season. And then they'd find out the following spring that they wouldn't see those friends any more because their dad was traded.

Kids don't understand, but that's just the way baseball and sports are.

Here today, gone tomorrow.

NO PAIN, NO PAY

My program of working out over the years changed so much from when I first started pro ball.

Back then, truly, the only thing I did was play baseball to get in shape and stay in shape. Lifting weights was taboo, especially for pitchers.

You had to have flexibility, and the "experts" thought weight lifting was out of the question for anyone who needed to be flexible.

When I was a kid in spring training, I can remember standing next to Bob Gibson, throwing between starts after we'd both pitched in a split-squad game. We were on mounds that were side by side, and I was just firing the ball in there.

Gibby asked me, "Does your arm really feel that good?"

I said, "Yes, sir!"

And he said, "It won't after you've been playing for 15 years."

He was right... but it didn't take 15 years for it to feel bad.

In '76, we had a shortened spring training. I didn't get enough conditioning in, and I got some nerve damage in my shoulder.

I was 26 and I was worried. They flew me back to St. Louis and had some nerve tests done on me.

Then Stan London, our team doctor, basically told me that I couldn't hurt my shoulder any worse than it was. He said that if

I could tolerate the pain and pitch through it, progressively my arm would get better.

I had complete faith in Dr. London. If my life was on the line, I'd want him for my doctor.

So I pitched the whole season and ended up eight and 10. And I still started 32 games.

When the season was over, Dr. London sent me back in to have the same tests run. The same nurse was doing the same nerve tests on me, and when she saw me she said, "Weren't you in here earlier in the year? Didn't you hurt your arm then?"

I said, "Yeah, but they told me it wouldn't get any worse if I kept pitching."

She just looked at me like I was crazy and said, "But didn't it hurt all year?"

I said, "Well, yeah."

She just couldn't understand that. If your arm hurt when you did something, why keep doing it?

She didn't realize that if you don't pitch, you don't get paid. At least not the next year, when your one-year contract is up.

PUMPING IRON

After I hurt my shoulder in '76, that off season Steve Carlton, Joe Hoerner, Mike Shannon and I went pheasant hunting up in Iowa.

Carlton wasn't with the Cardinals any more. He was with Philadelphia, but he still lived here in the off season. He may have been the strongest pitcher in baseball. He was one of the first pitchers to lift weights.

While we were hunting, he told me it would be beneficial if I'd start lifting weights in the off season. He offered to get me on his program.

So I did. He and John Denny, another pitcher, set it up. They said, "Meet us over at our gym." And they meant it when they called it a gym. They said, "Hey, this is not a health spa. We work."

I was thinking, "How tough can it be?" I walked in this place and there were very few machines... but a ton of free weights.

And no one in Spandex.

When I first went to this gym, the guy who ran the place said, "I'll take you through the stations."

He was teaching me technique and what exercises I needed to do. The owner put me through the paces and I got through about three stations.

Steve Carlton and John Denny were watching me because they were way ahead in the cycle. I was working harder than I ever did before, and apparently I was as white as the T-shirt I had on.

I was physically spent already. And then I got sick to my stomach. So I excused myself to go to the bathroom where I promptly threw up breakfast.

I came walking out like I was still a stud, and they all were laughing at me. They said, "How do you feel?" I said, "I'm fine, I'm ready to work."

But I had to slow the pace down. I never told them that I got sick, but they knew exactly what went on.

When I went to spring training in '77, I was probably in the best shape I'd ever been in, strength-wise. And I won 20 games that year.

Every off season after that we went back to the same gym— until they finally went out of business.

There just wasn't enough Spandex there to support it.

A SWELL DIAGNOSIS

When I first started my off-season program, I woke up one morning and both of my arms were swollen. I couldn't put my watch on, my arm was swollen so big.

I was scared. I mean, really scared. So I called Dr. London and he said, "Come on by."

I'm a right-handed pitcher, but when I got there I showed him my left arm. He looked at it and said, "Well, what have you been doing?"

I explained my new conditioning program to him, and he said, "Nothing to worry about. Your body's producing fluid."

I said, "Thank you so much! My right arm's the same way, but I was afraid to show it to you."

Now, Dr. London doesn't laugh much. But he laughed when he heard that.

In the clubhouse at Busch Stadium, my locker was right next to the trainer's room, and Dr. London had an office back there. When he was on the way in to the trainer's room, he would always stop by my locker and say hi to me.

But when I had an appointment to see him about an injury, and I went into his office right there near my locker, it was always like the first time we'd ever met.

He was all business. He had to put his game face on, too.

Now, everyone's got an off-season conditioning program and a personal trainer.

When I started, I had one guy show me how to use the stuff my first day in the gym. That was it. That was my personal trainer.

So guys are stronger now, but they're probably wound a little tighter. You see a lot of stuff like ribcage injuries. When I played, I can't ever remember seeing a guy pull a ribcage muscle.

When I worked out with Steve Carlton and John Denny, they always did a lot of stretching. So that was always the last thing I did when I worked out.

Even back then, we knew that strength is no good without flexibility.

GENO

Sometimes I think that the fans think ballplayers just hang out with each other. What you have to understand is that all these people in the clubhouse were family.

Gene Gieselmann and I had such a great relationship. He was our trainer. He was there when I got there in '74. And when I left near the end of the '88 season, he was the only person left from my rookie year who still traveled with the team.

We'd meet for lunch every day on the road. And we'd frequent the hotel bar almost every night after a game, if it wasn't put off-limits by some manager.

People come and people go, but Geno was the one constant in the clubhouse the whole time I was there.

Trainer Gene Gieselmann... making a house call on Ricky Horton.

OZZIE, WILLIE AND THE CARDINAL WAY

I never felt that there was a pecking order or anything like that on our teams, where the stars only hung out with the stars.

If a veteran went out to eat with a rookie, the rookie never paid. The rookies were just learning the ropes, and back then they didn't have any money.

That's the way it was when I first came up in '74. It was a veterans' team and the veterans sort of hung out with each other. But if you were out with them and you all had a couple beers, the tab would be taken care of by the veterans.

And you learn that when you become a veteran, you do the same for a rookie.

That's what I admired about Ozzie Smith. He really took care of Willie McGee when Willie came up in '82. Quite honestly, Willie was so green when he started here.

And Ozzie took care of him and taught Willie about the game. And then a few years later, Ozzie did the same thing with Vince Coleman.

I guess what I'm talking about is a rite of passage. You pass it on, veteran to rookie. In our case, you teach them the Cardinal Way.

The Cardinal Way is based on fundamentals and playing hard every time you put on that uniform.

When you have the birds on the bat, that's the rite of passage for the Cardinals organization as a whole. It's like a legacy that's passed down over the years.

Pepper Martin and Ducky Medwick and Enos Slaughter and Dizzy Dean and Stan Musial and Red Schoendienst and Bob Gibson and Lou Brock and Ozzie Smith and Tommy Herr and Fernando Viña...

There's such a great legacy of playing the Cardinal Way.

RUNNIN' REDBIRDS

Modern baseball is more or less a slugfest.

I understand that times have changed, ballparks have changed. But if you look back, the only times the Cardinals have had great teams it's been run, run, run.

From the Gas House team of the '30s to the teams of the '80s when the Cardinals had great teams, it seems like they always had an aggressive leadoff hitter and a great stopper.

You need someone who starts it and someone who stops it.

You don't want to lose that aggressive, Cardinal way of playing baseball. That's the tradition. That's the legacy.

RAW TALENT

I saw a lot of Willie McGee in spring training in '82, after he was traded here by the Yankees for Bobby Sykes.

Whitey Herzog had me pitching a lot of "B" games because it took so long for my arm to get loose every spring. Normally, the "B" games were for the guys who were at the end of the 40-man roster, the guys who weren't supposed to make the team.

And Willie was in the "B" games when he came in, because they didn't expect him to start in center field for a World Series contender.

And he didn't. Not right away.

He had so much raw—and I do mean *raw*—ability. He was a switch hitter, and he'd swing at balls out of the strike zone from both sides of the plate. He was just a wild, free-swinging, raw talent.

I saw him a lot that spring, and he was good. But not good enough to make the team that'd had the best overall record in the '81 split season.

So he started the season at Louisville in Triple A. Then David Green, our center fielder, got hurt. Willie got called up in May and he just did everything.

He was still a wild swinger. But I'd heard that Whitey told the batting instructor, "Don't fool with Willie's swing. Just let Willie play."

And, boy, did he play.

AN "A" STUDENT

Willie McGee would always start conversations by saying, "I'm not the smartest guy in the world but..."

Yeah, not smart like a fox!

He retains everything that's told him. And that's important. Willie would make a great instructor or a great coach.

And he's just a genuine person.

I was in the dugout one time, standing next to Whitey, when Willie struck out. And Willie would have that comeback walk to the bench with his head down, that somebody-just-killed-his-puppy look.

I told Whitey, "If he feels that bad about striking out, imagine what he feels like at a funeral!"

It didn't matter if Willie had three hits in a row and we were ahead by 10 runs. He always felt that he let everybody down when he didn't get a hit.

But he'd strike out, and they'd throw him the same pitch the next time and he'd rake it for a base hit.

He would either adjust... or maybe the best expression is "cut off the head and let the body do the work."

Willie was one of the smartest players I ever played with. He studied the game so well.

He knew what needed to get done. If he didn't do it, as sensitive as he was, he'd over-think things. He had so much talent, but he was so over-sensitive if he looked bad up there at the plate.

Everybody on the team told him, "Hey, if you hit .300 you're still making seven outs out of every 10 at-bats."

The first year he led the National League, in '85, he hit .353. So he still made six and a half outs out of every 10.

But when you're as sensitive as Willie is, that's still hard to take. He needed to not think. He needed to let his ability take over.

LEARNING FROM WILLIE

Willie was so unselfish. He did whatever it took to win a game.

If we needed a ground ball to the right side—to move the runner from first base into scoring position—Willie hit a ground ball to the right side.

If there was a ball hit to center field with a runner on first, rather than take a questionable shot at throwing the runner out at third base, Willie would throw to second base.

That kept the batter at first base and kept the double play in order. And from a pitcher's standpoint, that's huge.

I know it really looks good when somebody can throw for show—and Willie had a good arm. But as a pitcher, I don't want a good throw to third base that doesn't get the guy out.

If it's not a sure out, the other team has runners on second and third, instead of first and third. So now they can get two runs on a single, instead of us getting two outs on a grounder.

*Tommy Herr... keeping the double
play in order (as Ozzie Smith watches).*

Especially when you have a defense like we had in the in-field. Ozzie Smith and Tommy Herr and Terry Pendleton turned a lot of double plays.

If you don't keep the double play in order, that's how big innings get started.

And Willie understood that.

It frustrated Willie when younger players didn't want to learn. I remember Willie when he was contemplating retirement, tell-ing me how much things had changed.

He was trying to explain to a young outfielder the importance of throwing to the right base—the importance of fundamental Cardinal baseball.

Willie was saying, "It has to be a sure a thing." And the young player, with an ego, was telling him, "But I had a chance to get him at him at third base."

And when Willie was trying to explain how to get a jump on a ball hit to the outfield, the same young player was telling him, "But my college coach told me to do it this way."

Willie didn't say anything more to the kid. Willie was too modest.

But the point is: who would you rather learn from? A college coach, or Willie McGee?

By the way, shortly after that, the kid was sent back down to the minor leagues.

WHEN IT'S TIME

Willie was here for over eight years. He left when they traded him in '90, then he came back here to play again in '96. And he never changed. He just went about his business.

He actually asked for my advice about retiring in the late '90s. I had been out of baseball almost 10 years, and he asked me, "When is it time to go?"

I said, "That's something you have to decide. But base it on two things: is the game still fun? And how do you feel about your performance?

"Don't retire if you think you can still play and you still like coming to the park. And don't make it a hasty decision."

And Willie said, "How will I know?"

And I said, "You'll know... you'll know."

He played a couple more years and did well. But he had signed a contract as a part-time player, and they were over-playing him.

Willie is Willie... how can he not be a fan favorite?

They'd had a lot of injuries in the outfield and had to use Willie to fill in for all the guys who got hurt. It was hard on his body.

So he finally retired after the '99 season.

A FAN FAVORITE

Being on the outside and watching Willie's career in the 10 years I was out of the game, it was amazing.

It didn't matter what team Willie was with—Oakland, San Francisco, St. Louis—Willie endeared himself to the fans. And the fans endeared themselves to Willie.

It's just neat to see how Cardinal fans react to certain players. But with Willie, it was something special.

Fans here in St. Louis respect people who just play hard and keep their mouths shut. Even though Willie tells you he's not the sharpest knife in the drawer, the fans here know better.

They know what he's meant to the Cardinals and to the city of St. Louis. And they know what they mean to him, because he's so appreciative.

And that's really neat.

WHITEY THE GM

Whitey Herzog came in to manage halfway through the '80 season. I had a three-year deal that was running out, and he asked me why I didn't have a contract for '81.

I said, "They wait till the season's over and then they negotiate."

I don't think Whitey knew how the Cardinal organization worked then.

He said, "Doesn't it bother you not having a contract?" And I said, "No, that's just how they do it here."

Then when he became the general manager late in the season, I was the first player he signed for '81. Except I didn't realize that at the time. My agent had negotiated with an interim Cardinals official.

The club brought me in to sign my contract, and somebody said, "Would you like to meet the new GM?"

I was just happy to have a new contract. To me, it didn't really matter who the new GM was.

Then Whitey came walking out.

A PLAYER'S MANAGER

That first contract that Whitey signed me to was the first one I'd had that was insured.

Baseball salaries were starting to rise, so a team would take out a policy in case you got hurt. And the insurance company put clauses in your contract to keep you from doing things that were risky.

The contract was full of "thou shalt nots" in there. They had clauses that you can't skydive, you can't go spelunking, you can't ski, you can't scuba dive.

And one "shalt not" was hunting.

Now, I knew I wasn't going skydiving. I wasn't going into any caves. And I wasn't going scuba diving. But I go hunting every winter.

And I told Whitey that. I said I wouldn't sign anything that said I couldn't hunt.

Whitey said, "Let me see that." He grabbed the contract and read that part and said, "That's stupid!"

He took a pen and crossed out the no-hunting part. He put his initials by it and told me, "Put your initials right there."

And it was a done deal.

What Whitey did with that contract, crossing out the no-hunting clause, was such common sense.

Baseball is your job, but you can't change your entire life.

That was one of Whitey's traits. He realized you were a person. He knew you had a family and a life away from baseball. That's why he was considered a player's manager.

I don't mean that the players ran the show. Oh, no. Uh-uh. Whitey was definitely in charge.

You knew he would always do what was best for the ball club. He paid well, within the confines of his budget. And if he had to trade two guys to save the money to sign one guy he wanted, he'd do it.

But he had the respect of the players. You knew he was watching your back.

That's why he wanted to sign me to a long-term contract. He knew that security was important to a player for family reasons. And he knew he was here long-term.

He was going to get all his ducks in a row. And he did.

SIGN LANGUAGE

I was pitching in Montreal once when Darrell Porter was catching for us. After we batted, we started back out to the field, and I just pointed at Darrell.

He thought I was pointing behind him, so I pointed to my shin. He thought my shin hurt, but I was pointing to show him that he only had one shin guard on.

When he realized what I meant, he just shrugged and ran back in the dugout and put the other shin guard on and ran back out to home plate.

And I was thinking, *"He's* putting signs out for *me?"*

Hey, catchers don't put signs down to tell pitchers what to throw. They only make suggestions.

The only person I didn't shake off was Ted Simmons when I first came up. He was a veteran and I was a rookie.

But after that, I felt that if I'm gonna lose, I don't want to lose with somebody else's ideas.

I don't want to come back to the hotel room and say, "Gosh darn, why did I throw that pitch?"

I want to come back to the room and say, "Gosh darn, why did I throw that pitch *there?"*

STEALING A PEEK

With the pitcher and catcher, the only time you have to worry about someone stealing a sign is when you have a runner on base.

Usually, it's when a runner is on second base. But I remember Lou Brock being able to do it when he was on first base. And Vince Coleman could do it from first base.

Both Lou and Vince would get such a big lead. They still couldn't see the catcher's signal, but they could see where the catcher set up for the pitch.

That's important, because no right-handed pitcher throws a breaking ball to the inside part of the plate on a right-handed batter. The guy would crush it.

So if the catcher sets up on the inside, which a good heads-up base runner will see, the pitch will be a fastball. And the runner probably won't go, because it's easier to steal on a breaking ball.

*Vince Coleman... a heads-up runner can
steal a catcher's sign to help himself steal a base.*

There is not enough time from when the catcher sets up inside to relay that back to the hitter.

So when Lou and Vince were on first base, they were stealing the location to help themselves steal bases, not to help the hitters hit.

CODE BREAKERS

Once base runners get to second base, it's easy for them to relay signs to the hitter. They have a lot of time from when the catcher puts down the sign and the pitcher goes into his delivery.

The catcher flashes three or four signs to throw off the runner. But all teams basically use the same thing.

You know that all through the minor leagues, it's usually "first sign," "second sign" or "third sign" that counts. You switch them every once in awhile through the course of a game.

But if you're out there long enough at second base, you can figure out which sign is the right sign and then relay that to the hitter.

Tommy Herr was really good at that when he was running at second base. He might turn his head one way for a fastball, the other way for a curveball—something the hitter can see very easily.

And it's got to be something so natural that the fielders don't know the runner is relaying the pitch to the hitter.

CODE MAKERS

Until Mike Roarke got over here as pitching coach, it was always "first sign," "second sign" or "third sign." Then he had us using the scoreboard when the catcher called pitches.

You used "odd" and "even" to decide whether it was first sign or second sign, based on what the ball-and-strike count was.

For example, if you had one ball and one strike, that added up to two—an even number. So you would use the second sign that the catcher put down.

Any ball-strike count that added up to an even number—two and two, three and one—meant that you used the second sign.

If the count was two balls and one strike, or three balls and two strikes, that added up to an odd number. Any odd number count meant you used the first sign the catcher put down.

The whole idea was that if you were a runner looking in from second base to figure out the sign, you couldn't do it. It changed from pitch to pitch.

It worked and it was fun, but at times it was hard to remember. For some.

DANDY DARRELL

Darrell Porter was the best and the funniest of all the catchers.

As he would put the signs down, he would look at them to make sure he had them right. Every once in a while, he'd change his mind and wave at you. That was his human eraser.

Then he'd look down at the signs he was putting down the second time till he got them right.

He didn't just do it to me. He did it to everyone.

When he'd wave off the first sign, I'd tell him, "You threw the eraser down on me!"

It'd make you laugh, and he'd laugh about it, too. But he really did call a good game.

He was just more thoughtful than other catchers!

We'll all miss Darrell Porter. He was fun to be around, and he was a real team player.

When Whitey got him, at the time I didn't understand why. We already had Teddy Simmons behind the plate.

But when Darrell was in the postseason with Kansas City, his track record was a winner. He didn't have a particularly good

*Darrell Porter and Kenny Dayley, two winners
at work against the Dodgers in the '85 playoffs,
confer on the mound as Ozzie Smith looks on.*

season in '82. But winning the Most Valuable Player award of the World Series just proved Whitey's reason for bringing him in.

In the postseason, Darrell rose to the occasion—as all great players do.

MEETING OF THE MOUND

If you're struggling on the mound, and the guys in the bullpen are warming up, the last thing you want to see is the second baseman, the shortstop or the first baseman coming out to talk to you.

Especially if the pitching coach has already been out there. He's just allowed one visit per inning to the mound. If a coach or the manager comes out after that, the pitcher has to come out.

So if the coach had already made his visit, it used to tick me off when the infielders came out. After a few years, you get the hang of why they're there. I mean, it's not coincidental that the manager comes to get you after the infielders are out there.

They're just wasting time for the guys in the bullpen to get loose. As soon as the relievers are loose, you're history.

So the infielders come out to slow you down. Somebody gave them a signal to go "talk" to you. And the signal from the dugout is usually this: somebody makes his hand look like a mouth that's moving.

The pitcher doesn't see that. You're too busy on the mound. But all of a sudden, you've got a host of friends out there.

They're talking, but nobody has any input that can help you.

Except for Keith Hernandez.

Keith was my favorite. When he came to the mound from first base, it wasn't necessarily a situation where you were coming out.

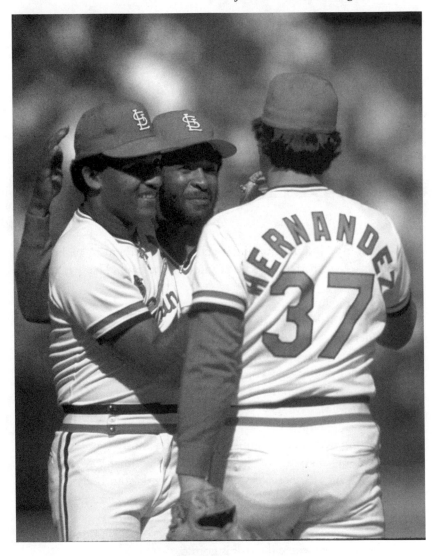

*Keith Hernandez... a visitor worth listening to
on the mound. Here he joins Joaquin Andujar (left),
and Ozzie Smith (center) in celebrating a victory.*

Keith was very astute about watching hitters hit. He knew how hitters should be pitched. Once in awhile, he'd come out and say, "I've been watching this guy, and this is how you can get him out."

He was really good about it. When Keith Hernandez talked out there, I listened.

ANATOMY OF A PROBLEM

I didn't mind the pitching coach coming out. I just hated the small talk when the infielders came over to stall. That's just a waste of time.

The pitching coach will say something when he gets there. He wants to slow you down, too. But it's not the same as the infielders.

They want to slow you down to get you out of there. A pitching coach wants to slow you down to keep you in there.

He may just want to break up the rhythm of the inning. Or sometimes he'll have suggestions for what he's seen from the dugout.

In my case, the pitching coach would mostly say, "You're rushing your body toward home plate." It's another way of saying that your arm position isn't in synch with your body. That affects your control—you're usually up in the strike zone—and your consistency.

When you're not doing what you always do in your delivery, you don't know where the ball is going.

Sometimes the pitching coach would talk about your arm position. He'd say, "Your elbow is dropping." If your arm goes down, your ball goes up in the strike zone.

Most of the time when your delivery is messed up, it comes from being tired.

Or you're too pumped up. If you've got too much adrenaline, your body goes too fast and you get out of synch.

You try to throw too hard. You're over-throwing.

Or you could be too tense. Bob Gibson had this expression that had to do with that. Actually, his expression had to do with being scared.

Gibby would say, "There's a nerve that runs from your rear end to your shoulder and on to your fingertips. And when the rear end tightens up, so do your fingertips."

KAATNIP

When Jim Kaat was with us, he had a theory about pitching coaches. It was more like a pet peeve.

He'd say, "If a pitcher throws a bad pitch or a number of bad pitches, the pitching coach goes out to the mound to correct him.

"But if the batter takes a couple of bad swings, you don't see the batting instructor running out to home plate to correct his swing.

"The batter is successful three times out of 10—at best. The batting instructor only talks to batters back in the dugout, after they've already failed.

"So why does that make sense?"

Jim never could figure that out. And neither could I.

NO LAUGHING MATTER

When you're on the mound, nobody has a sense of humor. You have to understand: the game's serious.

The only time I ever thought anything was funny about a pitching coach's trip to the mound was one night in New York.

It was real humid. I had a one-run lead with two outs in the bottom of the ninth, but the Mets had the bases loaded.

So Claude Osteen came out to the mound to talk to me. Teddy Simmons was catching and he came out, too.

We didn't have any real stopper at the time. But I was tired. I was done.

In that situation, the pitching coach always says the same thing: "How do you feel?"

When Claude asked me how I felt, I said, "Man, I'm *tired*."

He said, "Well, the manager sent me out to see how you felt."

I think the manager then was Vern Rapp. Anyway, Claude just turned around and went back to the dugout. It was like, "Bye!"

It was still humid. I was still tired. And I was still in the game. I looked at Simmons and said, "Teddy, what was that all about?"

He just said, "Well, I guess it's up to you. You better get this guy out so we can go have a beer."

The amazing thing was, I struck the next hitter out. I can't remember who it was, but I know he was left-handed.

I threw him a sinker that fooled him. I was so tired, that sinker was so slow that the guy couldn't hit it.

I made the pitching coach and the manager look like geniuses... by basically telling them that I needed to come out.

So I guess it was a successful trip to the mound!

NO-HITTING DUO

My brother got his no-hitter when he was with Houston. He got it against Atlanta, and it was after my first no-hitter but before my second one.

The night Kenny pitched his, we had a night game here in St. Louis. After our game a reporter told me about Kenny. As soon as I got home, I tried to call him to congratulate him, but I couldn't get hold of him till the next day.

When I finally got through, my little jab at him was, "It's about time you threw one!"

It was only a year after I got my first no-hitter.

The two things I am most proud of in my career are when we won the World Series in '82 and when Kenny and I became the first brother combination with no-hitters in the big leagues.

We're still the only brothers with nine-inning no-hitters.

The Niekros and the Perrys never did it. Daffy Dean did it but Dizzy didn't.

That's what my father was most proud of. He just missed seeing my first no-hitter and he didn't see Kenny's, either.

But that didn't stop him from telling people about it.

The Astros eventually traded Kenny to the Angels. He remained a starter but he never got another no-hitter.

So I bested him there!

But he made the All-Star team with the Angels, just as he had as a reliever with the Astros. So he's one of the few pitchers who was an All-Star in both major leagues.

I never made the All-Star team. So Kenny bested me there.

That's probably the one thing in baseball I never accomplished.

*With Kenny in May of '79... with our plaques from the Cardinals
for being the first brothers to throw big-league no-hitters.*

WORLD SERIES DEBUT

I started the opener of the '82 World Series and got my butt kicked.

I wasn't very good. That was the main reason.

But our scouts had followed the Brewers, and we had gone over all these reports that said, "The Brewers are all home run hitters and no speed. So play them here and play them there. Pitch them here and pitch them there."

It seemed like every ball was through the hole or caught where we couldn't throw anybody out. And it turned out to be an old-fashioned butt kicking.

When that game was over, I remember Ozzie Smith coming up the runway and saying, "Hey, we just need to play everybody the way we played guys all through the year. Forget the scouting reports."

And that's pretty much what we did the rest of the Series.

PRE-VICTORY PARTY

After I lost Game 1 at home, I pitched Game 5 in Milwaukee and lost again.

I pitched okay, nothing spectacular. Actually, Bruce Sutter came in because he needed a little bit of work, and he gave up a couple runs, too.

That put us down three games to two. We had to win the next two games back in St. Louis to win the World Series.

Game 5 was on a Sunday afternoon and there was an off day on Monday. We were on the flight home, and all of a sudden Bruce said, "Party at the Forsches' house!"

I couldn't believe it. I'd just lost two of the biggest games of my life. I said, "Bruce, this is a bad idea."

But Bruce was telling everybody in the back of the plane, "Party at the Forsches'!"

I said, "No!"

Well, by the time the wheels landed in St. Louis, there was a party at the Forsches'. Whitey didn't know—thank God we were in the back of the plane.

I guess Bruce figured everybody needed to relax. He picked our house because it was the best venue. We had a basement with a full bar.

The thing I was afraid of was: Here I was, losing Game 5, and all of a sudden there's a party at our house. What if I'm the reason we lose Game 6 and the World Series, too!?

The party started about nine o'clock on Sunday night after Game 5.

The majority of the team showed up. Guys brought their wives and we all had a great time.

Whitey had scheduled an optional practice for Monday, which means you didn't have to go. And I didn't. There had to have been some bad heads on Monday. I know I had one of them.

But when we played the Brewers again on Tuesday, we blew them away. That was the rain-delayed game that John Stuper pitched.

It seemed to me that Bruce was right. Everybody was pretty relaxed.

So the Series was even at three games apiece. Then we went into the pressure of Game 7. The World Series came down to one game—as it did again in '85 and '87. We just fared better in '82.

Who knows? Maybe we should have had a party at the Forsches' for the other two!

Unfortunately, the other two were on the road.

*Our fans partying after we clinched the '82
world championship... we partied three days earlier!*

VOICE OF THE CARDINALS

Jack Buck was here for my whole life in St. Louis.

You talk about what is a professional broadcaster? They should have his picture next to it in the dictionary.

He was just so good in interviews, always making you feel comfortable and at ease. He treated you the same way, whether you were a rookie just coming to St. Louis or a veteran who had just been traded away.

When he interviewed you before a game, he had his tape recorder and his stopwatch. He always started by saying, "Three, two, one..."

Then he'd press his stopwatch and say, "This is Jack Buck."

He'd do the interview, never look at the stopwatch, close the interview, push the stopwatch—and it would always be within five seconds of when it should be done.

I never remember having to tape one over with him. When we were through, he'd always show you the stopwatch. And have a little chuckle.

That's how good Jack Buck was.

With the passing of Jack Buck, Mike Shannon is the only constant for people my age who listened to the Cardinal broadcasts.

After all those years of doing the games together, Mike is pretty much *the* Cardinals broadcaster now. Regardless of who comes after Jack.

It used to be Buck and Shannon. Now it's Mike and whoever's sitting next to him. That's not a slam on anyone who has been next to Mike or will be in the future.

I just don't think it will ever be the same.

FIRE ALARM FRENZY

Everybody in baseball knew who Jack Buck was. He always made himself available at the ballpark.

I know for a fact that when I was traded to Houston, he was respected there. I'm sure that's how he was viewed with all the ball clubs.

People just loved his sense of humor. There's nobody who could work a banquet like Jack Buck. I never heard him be unfunny. Or tell the same joke twice.

One of the funniest things I remember happening with Jack Buck was in real life.

We were on the road and the fire alarm went off in our hotel in Philadelphia. It was about 3:30 in the morning.

They had these speakers on each floor for emergencies, and a really loud voice came through telling us to exit the hotel.

The first thing I thought of was, "Put your clothes on and get down to the street as quick as you can!"

I got down there and we were all standing around in front of the hotel. I saw Jack Buck, and he was wearing these very nice, tailored pajamas. I thought, "I got here in a hurry, but I still had time to put my clothes on."

I went up to Jack and said, "I see you didn't have time to dress for the occasion."

And he said, "When they tell me to get out of the room, I'm getting out of the room!"

His wit and his loyalty to St. Louis are what made him as special as he was.

GOLFING LEGENDS

This is one of the neatest things that happened to me when I got done playing.

Jack Buck, knowing that I love to golf, asked me if I'd be interested in playing a round with his group. He said, "We only play nine holes." And I said that was fine.

Fine? I got there, and our foursome was Jack Buck, Stan Musial, a friend of theirs and myself. Fun? Oh, my gosh, I was floating!

I was so excited that I was picking up their clubs for them, like a little kid who idolized those two legends in St. Louis.

When we finished playing, Jack said, "Would you like to join us for a sandwich? Enos is joining us."

So I was sitting there having a sandwich with Stan Musial, Hall of Famer; Jack Buck, Hall of Famer; and Enos Slaughter, Hall of Famer.

I don't even remember the conversation. It was seventh heaven, just to be in their company. What fan wouldn't have loved trading places with me?

I just sat there thinking, "Life is good."

SEA OF RED

Throughout baseball, fans in general are measured now against Cardinal fans.

Through the success the Cardinals have had through the years, and the nationwide TV exposure, and things that out-of-town broadcasters have said, our fans at Busch Stadium are the measuring stick for every ballpark.

First of all, you have the Cardinal Red thing. Everybody wearing red to the ballpark every game is absolutely awesome.

You can see it on TV when they pan around the ballpark. But it's not the same as if you're on the mound, seeing it in a circle all around the stadium.

If that doesn't get the adrenaline up and get you pumped, I think you're dead!

It just makes your performance level much higher. You can't go out there feeling your best physically and mentally every day.

When you see the ballpark filled every game, with everybody wearing red, it just brings you to another level.

CARDINAL FANS, YOU'RE NO. 1

You see fans go crazy at other parks, like fans in Anaheim when the Angels won the World Series. But that's once in 40 years.

Cardinal fans show up when the team is good, bad or indifferent.

And knowledgeable? Our fans don't just appreciate it when a Cardinal makes a good play. If someone on the other team makes a good play, our fans will clap for him, too.

Hey, in some ballparks, if a visiting player makes a good play the fans boo him!

Our fans love the Cardinals, but they love the game, too. They just appreciate a good performance by both teams. They like to see the game played right—the Cardinal Way—whether the player is actually a Cardinal or not.

A good example was when Mark McGwire was here going for his 500th career home run. The Padres came in, and Tony Gwynn was going for his 3,000[th] career hit.

The fans gave ovations to both players whenever they came up. Tony didn't get his 3,000[th] hit here that series, but the fans appreciated everything he had done in his years in San Diego. And they appreciated what kind of person he was.

They really wanted to see Tony's 3,000[th] hit. They didn't want to see it at crunch time to beat us... but they wanted to see it!

A LITTLE PIECE
OF THE PARK

When we were in the '82 World Series, Cardinal fans hadn't seen their team get that far since '68.

When we clinched Game 7 at Busch Stadium, the security people had this show of power that was almost a joke. They had police on horses on the field to keep fans from running out of the stands.

When Bruce Sutter threw that last strike past Gorman Thomas, the fans still got on the field shortly after the players left the dugout. So much for the cavalry!

Everyone knew that the artificial turf was worn out, and that the club said it would tear it up and replace it after the season.

The fans wanted a souvenir piece of turf. But you can't pull out plastic grass. You have to cut it.

So the game ended and we went into the clubhouse to celebrate. All my family was here—my dad and stepmom came in from Sacramento, and my cousin Ernie and his wife Naomi, everybody.

They were all waiting in the hallway outside the clubhouse. So I took a couple bottles of champagne out to celebrate with them.

When I got there, the paramedics were wheeling this guy by on a gurney. He saw me in my uniform and made them stop. All he wanted to do was congratulate us on winning the world championship.

I thanked him. And as they wheeled him away, I asked the policeman who was following them what happened. He explained that the guy was using a knife to cut up the turf and had sliced his leg.

It was a real deep cut and the guy was bleeding all over the place. But he was so inebriated that he didn't realize he had cut himself.

And when somebody told him and the paramedics came for him, he didn't really care. He had his little piece of turf with him.

Personally, I think that's a bit much. Even for a Cardinal fan.

THE EX-CARDINAL

After I got traded to Houston, the Cardinals were nice enough to honor me before the first game of my first series back here with the Astros.

The Cardinal fans gave me a big ovation.

Then I pitched against the Cardinals the next night. To hear my name announced for Houston as the starting pitcher and to be cheered again, it was just an unbelievable feeling.

It happened for Willie McGee and other players who left and came back with other teams. The fans here don't forget you if you did well as a Cardinal.

And that really makes you feel appreciated. That's the best compliment a player can get.

The best... especially coming from the best fans in baseball.

TIME FOR ME TO GO

I was 39 when I got out of baseball, and it wasn't because my arm was gone.

I was still healthy. I didn't throw hard, and my arm would bounce back. It just didn't bounce back as quickly as it used to.

I could have kept pitching. I could have bounced here and bounced there.

But when I was young and I'd lose, I always had confidence in my ability. I always thought I'd win the next game, and I always knew when the next game would be. I usually started every fifth day.

When I reached the end of my career, losses became harder because I didn't know when my next chance to pitch would be. Wins were harder to come by, and so were the number of times I pitched.

So when I lost, I didn't know when I could redeem myself. That's a bad feeling.

That's when you know you're done. And that's why it was pretty easy for me to retire.

Reaching out to Cardinals fans... who always reached out to me.

HOME ST. LOUIS HOME

Other than growing up in Sacramento with my Mom and Dad and brother Kenny, my best memories are here in St. Louis.

This will always be home. Playing here. Living here. Raising a family here. Making friends here. All of my life-long dreams were fulfilled here.

I came here in '74. I was traded in '88. I retired in '89. And now, over the years, I think the fans probably remember me as better than I was.

I appreciate that too, but I know what I did. Statistics don't lie! I know I was fortunate to be here on three World Series teams.

I think fans appreciate that, even though I was along for the ride.

Now I'm a fan.

I'm out there cheering for the Cardinals, too. And I'll always cheer for them.

But I don't know if I qualify as one of the best fans in baseball. Because if the Cardinals are winning, I'm an even better Cardinals fan!

When I go to the ballpark now, it's fun to sit in the stands. The view is great and so is the atmosphere.

But after all my experiences in the dugout, I have to tell you... it's still the best seat in the house!

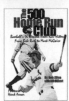